style on a shoestring

style on a shoestring

ANDY PAIGE

New York Chicago San Francisco Lisbon London Madrid Mexico City
Milan New Delhi San Juan Seoul Singapore Sydney Toronto

The McGraw-Hill Companies

Library of Congress Cataloging-in-Publication Data

Paige, Andy.
Style on a shoestring. / Andy Paige.
p. cm.
ISBN 0-07-149284-4 (alk. paper)
1. Women's clothing. 2. Fashion. 3. Shopping. I. Title.

GT1720.P35 2009
391'.2—dc22 2008033556

1 2 3 4 5 6 7 8 9 10 11 12 13 14 15 16 17 18 19 20 21 22 FGR/FGR 0 9

ISBN 978-0-07-149284-3
MHID 0-07-149284-4

Illustrations by Ben Ceccarelli
Interior design by Monica Baziuk

This book is printed on acid-free paper.

For David

Thank you . . . I love you!

Contents

Acknowledgments

FROM A CRAMPED two-bedroom home in Chickasaw, Alabama, with yummy homegrown vegetables, occasional government cheese, stacks of *Vogue* pattern books, lots of loving guidance, and daily lessons in Southern strength and charm, my mother, Beth, and my grandmother Judy taught me the skills and helped me build the confidence necessary to navigate the ultra wealthy and chic terrain of New York's fashion industry, looking like a million without spending a fortune. My skill, my flair, my backbone, and my down-to-earth approach to all of this paint and panache—I owe to you both!

Mom, I could not be happier to have the opportunity to thank you. You taught me by your exquisite example that beauty, style, and grace are skills, learnable by all and not exclusive to the elite. Thank you for your encouragement, strength, sense of pride, and unending love.

I want to thank my loving grandmother, Mammaw as I call her, for reinforcing my mother's economic sophistication by making my clothes and teaching me to sew. Mammaw, I appreciate all of your sacrifices and selflessness. I love you.

Rhonda Britten, founder of the Fearless Living Institute (fearlessliving.com), has been a guiding light and a source of immeasurable inspiration and self-awareness. This book could not have been written without her. Rhonda, thank you so much for seeing me—really seeing me and understanding, believing in me, encouraging me, and illuminating the path to my dreams.

An endless bucket of thank-yous goes to my incredible literary agent, June Clark, and my huge-hearted editor, Johanna Bowman. Thank you for your patience, understanding, and unwavering dedication to me and *Style on a Shoestring*.

I thank my dad, Mike; bonus mom, Andrea; and my sisters, Maria, Elena, and Lucy, for their acceptance, love, and understanding. Your love means the world to me.

Thank-yous and winks to my angels, my Pappaw, my Pop, and my twin sister, who have passed but who send me daily reminders that I am on the path of my true purpose. Thanks for the pennies, Pappaw. I love you, too!

To Amy Green, my sweet high school partner in crime who is now director of distribution for my business, Cents of Style, you will always be my BFF. I thank you for your love and support after all of these years.

I also want to acknowledge Mary-Ellis Bunim and John Murray of Bunim-Murray Productions. Thank you for "Starting Over." Your impact is infinite.

And finally, to Beegs—thanks for stopping!

Introduction

FINALLY—I AM so excited to tell you everything I know (well, almost!). Fashion, beauty, and all things delightfully budgetary have been a passion of mine for years. As a young girl growing up in a small town in Alabama, I was taught the importance of femininity and sophistication from early on. Now I know "Alabama sophistication" may seem like an oxymoron, like jumbo shrimp or right-wing liberal, but I was taught by example. Both my mother and my grandmother worked very hard to tame my wild ways and teach me the importance of looking the part, even if you didn't have a pot to piss in.

My grandmother (Mammaw) made almost all of my clothes when I was a young girl, and this really allowed my fashion imagination to flourish. We would go to the fabric store and pore over stacks of pattern books, looking for something that we both liked. Then once we had the canvas, we could paint with any fabric and trim that we could dream up. Mammaw always made dressing an event, and the anticipation of slipping into one of her creations was thrilling.

Though my mom didn't sew, she was and still is the epitome of Southern grace, charm, and polished perfection. I was skillfully instructed on skin care, makeup, hair care, and appropriate accessorizing as a rite of passage, and from the day of instruction on, I was expected to present myself like a lady every morning. Of course, I went through a rebellious stage with dyed black hair and a horrible asymmetrical permed do (eek!), but I always respected my mom's incredible style and her drive to avoid having me be perceived as lower class.

I confess the sale rack was the only rack we shopped, and dumpster diving behind the fabric store for discarded creative goodies provided memories I cherish. Mom had a way of blending things to make them look rich, and Mammaw had the skill to whip up a Chanel replica in an afternoon. Together they carved the understanding that you simply do not have to pay a lot of money to look beautiful or to be perceived as educated, celebrated as stylish, or touted for your grace and femininity.

Now, while I was wallowing in my own personal Tennessee Williams Southern sugar bath, God decided he was going to give me an incredible gift. You should know I say God gave this to me, but Mammaw swears it was her collard greens. The gift was just mine, no one else's, and with this gift I could do almost anything. By the age of ten, I had grown to be five feet eleven inches . . . Do I have to tell you what happened next? Yep, by the time I was seventeen, I was a seasoned working model in New York City, making my way, keeping my nose out of trouble, and building on the skills of home.

While I was in the holding room of my modeling agency one day, my booker called me back and took my measurements. By absolute accident, we discovered that I was the exact measurements for a JCPenney tall fit model. She asked if I knew what a fit model was and then briefly explained that a fit model worked with designers to help create clothes that fit the body perfectly. Immediately afterward, she sent me over to a client to fill in for a missing model. At that time, JCPenney set the sizing standard in the industry, so my measurements and my knowledge of sewing and garment construction landed me the opportunity to work with more than forty designers over eight years, helping them create beautiful silhouettes around my frame.

This work is certainly not the glamorous part of the modeling industry, but the lessons I learned and expertise I gathered have served me immensely. I understand how to *fit* a body—any body—like none other, and great fit is half the battle of looking like a million without spending a fortune. After thousands of garments and hundreds of different styles, I learned that beautiful fit is a constant. Styles will come and go, and designers will dish up new duds each season, but what looks the most flattering on a figure will never change. Can I get an *Amen*?

After years as a successful model and trained makeup artist and with a couple of degrees in media studies and broadcast journalism, I thought the progression to TV seemed logical, but it proved much harder than I had expected. Becoming the beauty and style expert on NBC's Emmy-winning daytime reality drama "Starting Over" was an amazing turn of events that allowed me the opportunity to utilize all of my talents and offer up my personal brand of thrifty chic know-how on a public stage. Through that opportunity and the overwhelming response from millions of viewers, my business, Cents of Style, was born.

Style on a Shoestring presents my loving Cents of Style formula—a true system—of how to create incredible style on a hair-thin budget. This formula can be applied to every body type and income level, as style has no boundaries, ladies. I will walk you through the same steps I take with my private clients and the dozens of ladies I have made over on TV. So in effect, you can consider this book a workbook for creating your own makeover!

Know that amazing change takes amazing courage, and as you read this, remember I am talking to you—and yes, you can do this. The most frustrating facet of my work is convincing women of how absolutely beautiful they are and of all the potential they hold. We gals are exquisite creatures, ripe with the power of femininity and volcanic with the bubbling of creative flair just under the surface. We tend to talk ourselves out of true fabulousness, and I want you to push through. Prepare yourself for the inspired *frugalicious* eruption.

If you follow the guidelines for better undies, you will find yourself with higher hooters. (Woo-hoo!) If you dedicate a Saturday to cleaning out your closet, you will discover where you are "style stuck." If you follow my shopping guidelines, you will save hundreds of dollars on your wardrobe. And if you apply my Cents of Style Color Formula, you will be accessorizing like a "Sex and the City" thrifty diva!

This is your key. Change is rustlin' in the following pages, and it's calling your name. If you have any questions or need more personalized help, you can always reach me by visiting my website (centsofstyle.com). I'm here for you—so let's get started.

style on a shoestring

You Don't Have to Spend a Fortune to Look like a Million

1

YOUR IMAGE IS important. It is *very* important! We can pretend that people should look past the superficial to see us for who we truly are and convince ourselves that we want to associate only with folks who value the goodness of our heart, not the label in our britches. But let's be honest; that is a steaming pile of hooey. How you look—the visual package you present—is a crucial element in achieving your goals, building self-esteem, establishing relationships, and attracting the love you want.

Your image reflects your moxie and modern spirit. It tells the world about your creativity, productivity, confidence, and direction. Frustrating but true: how you look tells the world how to treat you, because it indicates how you treat yourself. *Sigh* . . . I feel your pain, Hot Stuff.

I know you want to turn heads when you walk into a room, have your friends proclaim your astonishing style, and approach every day with the confidence that what you put on will signal the masses that you are a magical force of individuality. We all want that scrumptious feeling of fashion euphoria experienced when we have on something so perfect it makes us feel like a different person—a stronger, more confident, glowing person. That is the spell cast by great style. But here is the deal. Great style is a skill, not a privilege! (Can I get an *Amen*?)

When you understand your body type, fit principles, shopping strategies, and the best times to shop for everything, achieving a great Cents of Style is a snap! Honest. I promise. Throw in a few exercises to build your style muscles, and you have a thrifty diva in the making! And this goes for women of every shape, size, and shade.

If you read the good-humored, realistic advice I lovingly dole out on my website (centsofstyle.com), you know that I am talking to you—the woman who hates her tummy or wishes she had better boobies, dreams of a firmer butt or thinks she has fat arms, likens her legs to tree trunks and speaks of her thighs using the term *thunder.* Perhaps the sixth-grade bully's taunting words still haunt you when you're getting dressed, and you generally feel dizzy from the emotional cocktail of some or all of these perceptions.

You are me; you are we—the glorious mass, united when it comes to being self-critical and thinking we don't have what it takes to be super fabulous. Thanks to advertising and the way that women are represented in the media, we all have incredibly ridiculous standards to live up to. Yep, thanks to you, media machine! Heaven forbid you would support us in feeling great about ourselves; whatever would you sell us?

Well, the following pages are injected with thrifty-chic mojo, and I want you to eat it like a piping hot box of Krispy Kreme doughnuts. Enjoy learning the secrets of the fashion industry that trick you into spending more, ways to make a five-dollar thrift store find look like a five-hundred-dollar designer deal, and the wardrobe-building strategies that will have you spending less, looking better, and being prepared for the local baseball game, exciting first date, business meeting, or holiday soiree.

Fashion and great style are the ultimate social equalizer. Whether you are sporting a five-hundred-dollar department store suit or a fifty-dollar consignment shop steal, visually selling a polished, pulled-together look is a feat we all crave. But let's face it, more of us have a dime than have a dollar, and those of us with dimes want to look just as good as those with dollars. Great style, just like any skill or talent, is the result of a little effort and study, not affluence and money.

In fact, no matter what our bankbook indicates, I have yet to work with a client or meet a gal who didn't enjoy spending less. The desire for a bargain unifies us all, and there is nothing to be ashamed of. Thrift is a beautiful thing. *Style on a Shoestring* is for every woman who wants to look her best, understand how to fit her body, shop with cunning expertise, organize her closet to optimize every garment, and never spend another dime on a frock that lives only in the closet and doesn't enjoy the glory of being draped on her hot bod.

It is important to recognize that an empowering style can be enjoyed by everyone, not just the skinny-minnies, ladies who lunch, or dames with great gay boyfriends and deep pockets. We all want to look and feel our best, and certain beauty and style principles are universal. A great Cents of Style is all about femininity and delightfully shrewd style, not a trust fund and personal shopper!

Femininity is the greatest power we have. In fact, it is the most powerful thing in the universe, it comes in all shapes and sizes, and best of all, it's *free*!

When you look at the most powerful and influential women throughout time, one common thread is an acute awareness and use of their femininity. Think of Cleopatra; Queen Elizabeth I and II; Yulia Tymoshenko, the most adored and powerful leader in Ukraine and the former Soviet Union; Jacqueline Kennedy; Ann Richards, the former governor of Texas; and Nancy Pelosi, the first female Speaker of the House of Representatives. These women are known for celebrating the distinction of great style and femininity. When you combine strong femininity with thrifty-chic know-how, you are simply unstoppable!

The confidence of shopping wisdom and the sublime understanding of how to rock your form with flair can make you downright drunk with power. (Woo-hoo!) So continue reading at your own risk. You may never get dressed the same way again. Awesome, huh? Let's get started!

In this book, we're going to explore a wide range of thrifty-diva topics. We'll start by discussing the crucial importance of the perfect-fitting bra and other undie wisdom in Chapter 2. Chapter 3 will show you how to find the right fit and style for your body type for everything from pants to tops to the dreaded swimsuit (breathe!). Avoid the most common fashion mistakes, outlined in Chapter 4. Chapters 5, 6, and 7 will serve as your shopping and organization guides. Navigating the sale rack becomes a cinch once you know what to look for and when to look. At this point, you'll want to know how the right colors and the right accessories can instantly update and add value to any outfit; Chapters 8 and 9 will reveal everything you need to know. In Chapter 10, we'll cover dressing on a budget for a big night out. And in Chapter 11, I'll leave you with some words of wisdom.

Once you've read this book, you'll have the tools to give yourself a complete makeover without breaking the bank. But what can you do right now? And where should you start? Here I've included some of my most basic tips for an instant wardrobe update. You can start to change your look in the morning, right now even. No dough required. Here we go.

FREE! FREE! FREE! FIVE KEYS TO LOOKING FABULOUS THAT DON'T COST A DIME EXTRA

With a wide-eyed understanding that comfort is the sun sign of most of our fashion zodiacs, I want to give you five simple, highly effective tools that will deliver a style boost to anything and everything you wear. These five tools, if used every day, will not in any way affect your budget but will visually elevate what you have on and send a modern message of fashion savvy.

1. You Have to Wear Lipstick Every Day

Yep, step one is lipstick. We all have it, but we forget what an impact it can make. It immediately brightens your face, whitens your teeth, and makes you look younger. Even if the only cosmetic you have on is lipstick, you will easily pull off a more chic, polished look.

As we age, many of us tend to choose darker, muddy colors, and I want you to avoid that. We lose the fullness of our lips over time, and dark lipstick only highlights that loss. Choose your favorite color of lipstick, and move up a shade or two in brightness. A brighter, lighter color will always look more youthful. So c'mon, this one's easy—paint your pucker.

2. Whatever You Have On Must Create Shape Through the Waist

Studies in the laws of attraction and social power have clearly shown that women who have a smaller waist relative to their hips naturally appear more attractive and powerful. This means that if you are hiding under shapeless sweats, boxy blouses, and swing jackets, you are giving all of your feminine power away.

Your tops and jackets *must* contain either shape-creating darts and seaming or a percentage of Lycra or spandex that helps the fabric skim the body. This principle means you need to make sure that your "girls" are sitting high and proud, so your tops and jackets have the chance to enhance your hourglass. There is plenty of bra advice in Chapter 2. This dynamic fashion step will modernize your look in an instant.

3. You Must Wear Cute Shoes

Clunky man shoes are a fashion albatross. With all of the adorable comfy options stacked high on the sale racks, there is just no excuse for sporting clodhoppers. A feminine, colorful, even playful shoe speaks volumes about your style and puts a spring in your step.

When choosing shoes, look for a feminine heel and toe, and opt for something that reveals as much of your foot as comfortably possible. This, of course, doesn't apply to boots, but a shoe that reveals more of your foot will make your legs look longer and your outfit more modern. And why not choose a colored or patterned shoe? Adorable leopard flats, gold sandals, or green pumps all tell the world you've got style. So . . . pretty packages for your tootsies are a must.

4. Your Handbag Is Your Social Barometer: Choose Wisely

The days of matching shoes and handbags are over. Today your handbag tells the world who you are, where you are going, and what you need to have when you get there. This single accessory can change the entire mood of your outfit and offers a style boost like none other.

Go for a bold color, and skip the black box with straps. A modern bag should celebrate what you like and not especially what you have on. Don't squander this ripe opportunity to make a big style statement. Push yourself into something bold, and you are sure to seem saucier.

5. You Must Incorporate Something Unexpected into Your Outfit Every Day

Your outfit must include something unexpected, which means you work the juxtaposition of textures, colors, patterns, and the tones of your garments. Building a little intrigue into your outfit is how you start to build style muscles. Going against the grain and having the courage to do the opposite of what would match or be expected can be both youthful and sophisticated.

For example, you could sport beautiful yellow accessories with a cobalt-blue dress instead of trying to match the blue perfectly or just wearing silver; add a few strands of pearls to your old, worn graphic T-shirt to give it a sophisticated edge; or choose a great walking shoe in red and wear it with everything. These creative expressions add visual interest and spark conversation. Adding a little something askew will reflect an adventurous spirit and will immediately add youthful modern play to everything you wear.

Are you ready to find out more about how to become a full-fledged thrifty diva? I want you to read this book with an understanding that these pages and principles apply to you whether you are a size 2 or 32, you make $25,000 a year or $250,000 a year, or you have big boobies or a big bum. I am talking to you. Now, let's start with the basics. Read on to find out about the Cents of Style foundation for a great outfit.

Bras, Undies, and Other Pick-'Em-Up, Suck-It-In Tools

2

EVERY GREAT MAKEOVER starts with the right foundation. We can't even begin to talk about building your dynamic thrifty-chic wardrobe until we address your underwear. The perfect-fitting bra and undies are key ingredients of the money-saving, style-boosting stew. Foundation garments are the building blocks for creating the shape you want out of the shape you have. I have always joked that I refuse to diet; I just wear higher heels and better bras and panties, and I immediately look ten pounds thinner. Today's undie options can have you prancing around like Jessica Rabbit while still feelin' as comfy as Lucy Goosey. You just need to know what to buy and how to find the right size for you.

In this chapter, I'm talking boobies, buns, and bellies. Let's not mince words; this is the trifecta of a winning shape, and we all struggle with these areas. We want to manipulate one or all of these regions to look bigger or smaller, higher or, well, higher, depending. The great news is that fabric technologies and shapewear designers have been working overtime to create comfortable, breathable jiggle managers that help us breeze through our day with confidence. Today's shapewear isn't the girdle/scuba suit of old, and the current bras on the market have been engineered like the space shuttle. So if you haven't shopped for new undies in a while, you will be amazed at the better body you can create in the lingerie department.

So how does having the right undergarments save you money? When your body is well shaped, everything you wear will look better, offering implied value. The goal of most gorgeous high-end clothes is to create a powerful image and feminine shape. So if we are going to fool the eye into thinking that our budget duds are designer dress, we need to start with the best shape possible. A forty-dollar bra will make a ten-dollar tee look amazing, but a ten-dollar bra will do very little to make a forty-dollar blouse look pricey—get it?

THE PERFECT-FITTING BRA

The right bra can lift both the girls and your spirits lickety-split. There is nothing more delightful than slipping into your favorite sweater or top and discovering the new waistline that your "better" bra has created. Ultimately, your bra keeps the girls perky, yes, but it also creates more shape and definition in your waist. It's a known fact that the higher your boobies, the smaller your waistline and the better posture you will have. Let's face it: in addition to all of these fabulous bennies, the other outcome of wearing a better bra is more confidence. Your clothes will look better, and you will feel better in them.

In a recent poll on my website (centsofstyle.com), a whopping 43 percent of women said they are living in uncomfortable, binding bras that won't stay put. Augh! How frustrating! Well, if you check a few points of fit and make some adjustments, it will help relieve your daily "boulder holder" burden. So, put on your bra, and get ready to give yourself a gander. It's time for a quick Fit Quiz:

- First, open the neck of your blouse. Go ahead: right now, look at the center front of your bra. Does it lie flat against your chest? Or is there a space between your body and the center gore (front band) of your bra? If there is a space, your cup size is not big enough, and I'll bet the underwire (if you have underwire) is poking you, because it is in the wrong place. The center gore of your bra has to lie completely flat against your sternum for a comfortable, proper fit—yes, completely flat!

- Do you have a double bubble? A definite sign of an ill-fitting bra is spillage. If you are pouring out of the top or spilling out of the sides of your bra, your cup size is all wrong!

- If you have an underwire, lift your arm, and feel for the outside cup seam or underwire track. If the underwire or side seam does not reach for the center of your underarm but falls shallow and more to the outside of your breast, your cup size is too small, and these bulging seams are probably rubbing you the wrong way. If shallow cup seams catch the tender part of your side and rub you raw all day, you need a bigger cup.

- Now go to the mirror, lift up your shirt, and turn around. Does the back of your bra ride up? If the back band is frowning, then your band size is too big, and one of two things is probably happening:

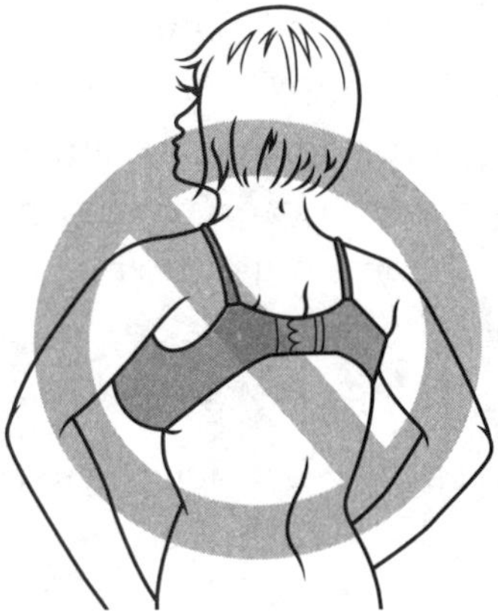

1. If you are smaller busted, your straps won't stay up.
2. If you are larger busted, your straps are digging into your shoulders because all of the weight of your breasts is being carried by the straps.

You have to understand that 70 percent of your booby support should come from the band—that's right, 70 percent! So you have to find the correct band size that stays put and completely balanced (level) all the way around your body. If the back rides up, you have lost the cup support, and your straps are more likely to fall or dig in.

IF YOU are a C cup or larger, you need to have a wider band—three hooks or better. If your band is flimsy and thin, it cannot support the weight of your bust, and it is probably riding up, digging in, and creating dreaded fat rolls as it crawls up your back. You need to find a band that is wider and offers more structural support.

The frowning in the back is also what causes back fat. A level bra won't pinch and gather the fat as it rides up. (Woo-hoo!)

- Finally, grab your straps from the top of your shoulders and lift. If you can lift your straps more than an inch off your shoulders, they need to be tightened. Loose straps offer no support and often won't stay put. Granted, only 30 percent of your support should come from the straps, but you need that 30 percent, so tighten 'em up.

Measuring for the Perfect Bra

You may remember the days when you were a wee tyke who needed new shoes and your mom would take you to the shoe store. Inevitably, a kind gentleman would come out and measure the width of your foot, the length of your foot, and the length of your toes. He would determine the exact size of your feet, go in the back, and return with a pair of shoes that fit like a glove. Well, shoe manufacturers realized that they could cut their inventory and overall costs by developing the medium shoe and force 75 percent of the population into it. It wouldn't be a perfect fit, but it was close enough that most people would deal with it, stretching their shoes and wearing them in.

Bra makers had the same bright idea some years ago. It used to be that you could find bras in dozens of sizes to fit all types of boobies and every booby need. But now most stores carry only a handful of sizes, and manufacturers have manipulated the sizing scale to fit their lack of inventory. As a result, the majority of us are wearing the wrong size, which means there is a pretty good chance the bra you have on right now isn't workin' for ya.

While shopping for the perfect childhood shoes may bring sweet thoughts of the past, I feel quite sure shopping for your first bra does not. Who wants to relive that horrible experience when you first started to "blossom" and your mom took you to get your first bra—yikes. Old Mrs. Whatsername came at your timid preteen frame like a buzzard on roadkill, poking and picking in a way that was so awkward and uncomfortable you wanted to run screaming from the fitting room. I can remember thinking, "Well, thank gawd that is over. That's my size, so now I will never have to do that again."

But the truth is that our breast size changes several times over our lifetime. With puberty, childbirth, weight loss, weight gain, a new workout routine, and menopause or other hormonal shifts, your breasts are affected. I recommend that women measure themselves twice a year. So I am going to teach you how to measure yourself *properly*, and I want you to commit to checking your bra size twice a year.

Measuring Your Chest. Bring a tape measure around your back, stand up straight, keep your arms down by your side, and measure just under your breast (top of your rib cage where your breast meets your chest). Make sure that the tape measure is level all the way around your body, and exhale. You want to ensure the measurement is just a wee bit snug. (**Note:** You may have to lift the girls to get the tape measure under there!)

If the number you measure is even, add 2 inches to it; if the number you measure is odd, add 3 inches to it. (So if your

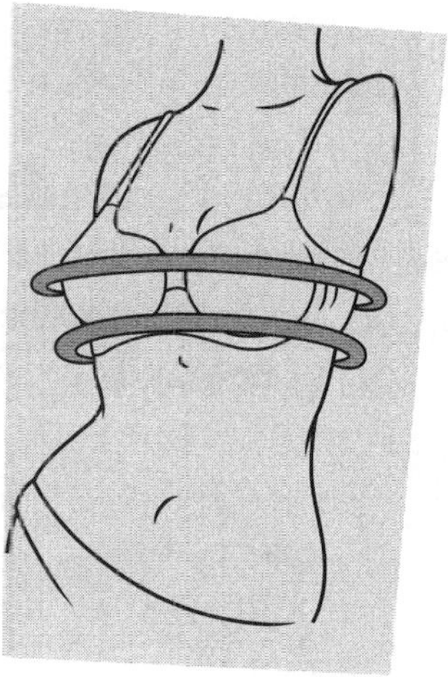

rib cage measurement is 35 inches, you would add 3 inches to make your bra band measurement 38 inches. If it is 32 inches, you would add 2 inches to make your bra band measurement 34 inches, and so on.) You have now determined your bra band measurement.

Understand that most current manufacturers suggest that you add 4 and 5 inches to your rib cage measurement. But as you will see, this makes your band too big, your cup size too small, and the total overall balance and comfort of your bra completely off. Again, you have to get the band right, or the function of your bra is kaput.

To determine your cup size, assume the same erect stance and measure around the apex (nipples) of your bust, the fullest part. If your nips are pointing south and not west, then you will want to take this measurement with your bra on. The difference between your apex measurement and your bra band measurement determines your cup size:

- 1 inch larger = A cup
- 2 inches larger = B cup
- 3 inches larger = C cup
- 4 inches larger = D cup
- 5 inches larger = DD cup
- 6 inches larger = DDD cup . . . and so on

You have now determined your correct bra size. (Yippee!) Most women who take these measurements discover they have just grown a cup size or two. I can assure you this measurement formula will offer you a much better fit. Keep in mind that your cup size simply represents the amount of fabric necessary to capture all of your breast effectively.

As you head out to purchase your new brassiere, remember that not every manufacturer's products are going to fit the same way. If you are a size 8 shoe and you try on twenty pairs of shoes, perhaps only half of them will fit you comfortably and work with your foot. The same is true with bras, so you have to try them on. Once you get them on, you will want to make some adjustments to achieve the optimal fit.

Bra Adjustments for a Better Fit. Fit your bra to the first row of hooks. This allows you to tighten with the natural loss of elasticity. You should not be able to pull the band more than a couple of inches away from your body when tugging at the back.

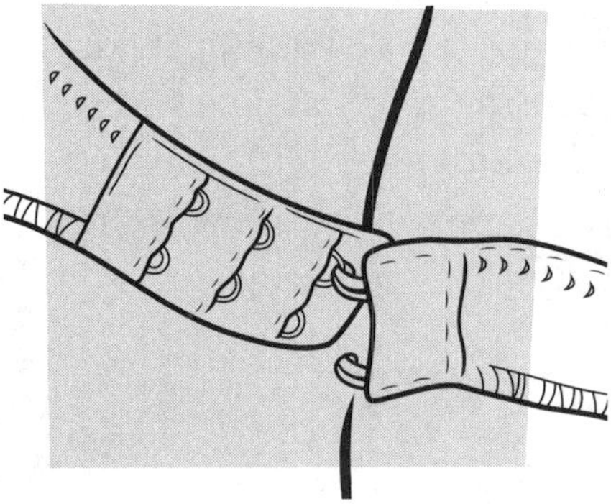

Adjust the shoulder straps so that your finger can run smoothly under the strap but the straps can't be lifted more than an inch off the shoulder. This is very important. If you can lift your straps off your shoulder more than an inch, your breasts need to be lifted and straps tightened.

When putting your bra on, bend over and pull all of the breast tissue from your underarm and underneath your breast to fill the cups completely. Many of us carry much of our breast tissue closer to our underarm, and this needs to be captured and contained in the cup.

Jiggle the wires into place, if your bra has them, so that they hug the body and cradle right under your breast.

The apex of your bust should fall halfway between the top of the shoulder and your elbow when you are looking in the mirror from the side.

Also make sure to get these details right:

- The underwire should end at the side edge of your body and lie flat against your sternum in the front.
- The side cups should hug your body.
- Everything must fit—not too tight and not too loose.
- There shouldn't be any wrinkles in the cup or anywhere else.
- The back band shouldn't ride up or bind.

What Bras You Need

All you need for everyday wear are two nude (the color of your skin) bras and one black bra. There is no reason to choose white bras, because white bras are unnecessarily noticeable under almost everything. In the "olden days,"

NEVER WEAR a white bra under a white shirt or, worse, a white bra under a black shirt. Nude will always create the illusion of invisible support.

white undies were a sign of cleanliness, but we all have regular access to soap and water now, so modern nude bras are a much better option. You should buy three new bras (two nude and one black) and remeasure yourself every six months to ensure proper support and fit.

You want to get your money's worth out of your bras, so each day, with your three basics, you should wash one, wear one, and let one rest. You should never wear the same bra two days in a row. The elastin in your bra has memory and needs to "rest" so that it can remember how to work. Think about it: when you wear your jeans two days in a row, they are usually much bigger on the second day. When you wash them, they shrink back down to size. The same is true for your bra.

THE WASHER and dryer break down the fiber and construction of your bras. Hand washing is best. Baby shampoo is very effective, gentle, and delightfully thrifty. It's perfect for all of your hand-washing needs.

Thrifty Bra Shopping

Bras and other foundation garments are the one type of clothing that's worth a little extra scratch. They give you a better shape, which can make thrifty clothes look richer. That said, I've found that keeping the stats of my favorite bra (brand, size, and style number) programmed into my cell phone comes in handy when I'm shopping discount and closeout stores. You never know when you will run across an unexpected closeout that has delivered your golden bra. I've found one of my favorite Wacoal bras at both T.J. Maxx and Big Lots on more than one occasion, and since I know *exactly* what I am looking for, a quick glance at the bra rack takes seconds and can provide huge savings.

Another bra cost cutter is to buy when department stores and manufacturers have their biannual lingerie events. In August and February, many bra manufacturers offer a buy-two-get-one-free-by-mail deal or a discount on your second bra of equal or lesser value. This is when you bag your bras.

I've also found that many department stores offer secret family-and-friend discount days a few times a year, and I always take advantage of this sale in the lingerie department. Some manufacturers *never* discount their bras, so a retailer discount is the only way to catch a break. To find out when your favorite bra goes on sale or has a manufacturer BOGO (buy one, get one), or when secret discounts may be available, just ask the sales help or manager of the lingerie department. Remember, everyone loves a bargain and wants to save money, so by asking, you are bonding with these store employees as thrifty divas.

Your Brassiere Options

No matter what your style or whether you want bigger boobies or bitty boobies, there's a bra for your every need. A bra wardrobe of sorts is something every woman needs, so you're prepared when you find that amazing twenty-dollar dress on the sale rack for the wedding you were just invited to. You should never have to walk away from a deal because you don't own the right brassiere.

Push-Ups. Push-up bras are the gold standard in optimizing your potential. Push-up bras incorporate a foam shelf at the base of your bra that offers an uplifting place of rest for your boobies and works to round them out and have them appear higher and fuller. A less expensive way to achieve this look is to add foam or silicone "cookies" or "cutlets" to bras you already own. This will help you achieve the look you desire without having to splurge on a whole new bra. Choose silicone cookies for a smoother line or foam cookies for more substantial lift and structure, and angle them in the groove of the underwire or cup seam for the best lift.

Minimizers. You can buy bras that capture and compress your breasts, making them look up to a full size smaller. When it comes to minimizing, uniboob should be avoided at all costs! You do not want to compress your breasts together and flatten them down. Choose a minimizer that contains each breast separately, offering full coverage with no spillage. All of the rules of proper fit apply to minimizer bras, especially the way the center gore fits. A cleavage-bulging center gore is the biggest mistake made by most women who wish to minimize. Aim for lift and separation (thank you, Jane Russell), with full coverage and compression of each booby.

Molded Bras. Don't be fooled: molded form does not mean padded. I have had this discussion with hundreds of women who are leery of the new molded (preformed) bras on the market. A padded bra is filled with old-fashioned batting (aka pillow stuffin'). Padded bras used to be the best option to dim "headlights" at the office and give yourself a little visual plumper. But today we have the modern molded form or foam-lined bra. These bras create shape without adding size and offer a smooth, seamless look under T-shirts and knits. They are also a perfect option for equalizing uneven boobies. (Yippee!)

Underwire or Tri-Panel Bras. If you are larger-breasted and hate underwire or can't wear underwire due to medical issues, you want to look for a tri-panel bra for optimal support and comfort. The construction of a tri-panel bra offers lift and reinforcement. The only downside is it's not seamless.

Additionally, larger busts benefit from rigid nonstretch straps. Elastic straps make larger boobies buoyant, and as the elastic starts to wear, Mother Nature wins the gravity battle, and the girls get sucked closer to the ground. A nonelastic strap or a strap with a smaller portion of elastic will add to the life of your bra and help keep the girls up and alert.

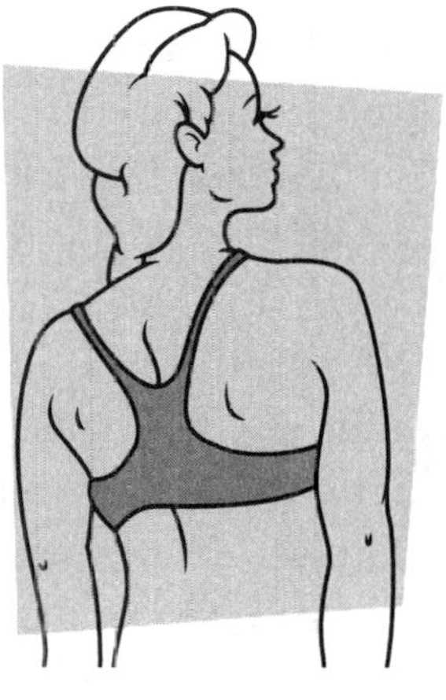

T-Back or Racer-Back Bras. T-back or racer-back bras are an excellent option for ladies with narrow shoulders, heavier-busted gals, and those of us who need a little help with our posture.

The T-back straps shift the weight from the edge of the shoulder to the center of the trapezius muscle, which is a long muscle that runs from the top of your shoulder all the way down the edge of the spine. This shift in weight distribution works to help keep you upright and your shoulders back. This is a very comfortable option for almost everyone; just be aware of peekaboo straps that might be present when you're wearing most scoopneck and V-neck tops or blouses.

IT'S CALLED *underwear* for a reason. Your bra wardrobe should include a nude racer-back or convertible bra that allows you to effortlessly wear any style top without tugging and shoving the straps back under your clothes.

Front-Closure Bras. Bras with a front closure usually create more cleavage, as they capture and push your bust forward and together, making mountains out of your molehills. The only drawback to a front-closure bra is that the band can't be adjusted as the elastic starts to wear out. So you'll sacrifice the extended life of these bras for pumped-up hooters, but this could be a small price to pay if you are going for a particular look. *(Wink!)*

Strapless Bras. A comfortable strapless bra is an oxymoron, like tight slacks, plastic glasses, or pretty sneakers. Strapless bras are notoriously difficult to find, fit, and wear. Though 70 percent of your support comes from the band, the strapless bra proves that you *really* need that extra 30 percent from the straps.

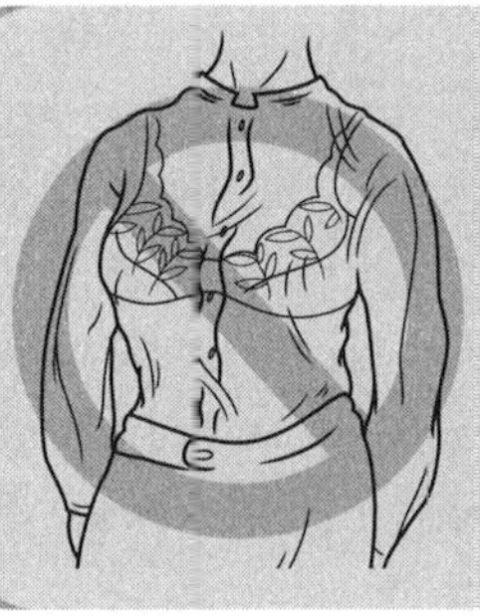

LACY BRAS are best for the boudoir and not blouses. If you can see the workings of lace either visually or texturally through your top, you need to change your bra.

When it comes to a better-fitting strapless bra, the band needs to be tighter and wider than usual. This may mean that you will need to go down in your band size and up in your cup size to achieve a stay-put fit. My favorite strapless foundation is actually a bustier. The long line of the bustier extends from your bust to your hip, creating an exaggerated waist shape and offering more lift and support. A smooth bustier usually works best for special-occasion dressing and most of your strapless-bra needs.

Duct Tape: Wonder Bra on a Roll. I can't leave the subject of strapless bras without talking about the wonders of tape. Yep, *tape*! Heavy-duty tape, usually duct tape, has been used by Hollywood insiders and catwalk strutters—like J-Lo in that plunging green dress at the Grammy awards a few years back—as a strapless-bra solution for years. The truth is, it's much cheaper than a strapless bra; duct can save you *dinero*. And you can go backless, plunge to your belly button, and create a jaw-dropping illusion your friends will corner you about as soon as you hit the ladies' room. But best of all, good tape simply works better.

First you need to make sure that your breasts and chest are clean, dry, and moisturizer free. This is not the time to go nuts with the cocoa butter; your skin needs to be degreased. You'll want to use six to eight strips of tape that are approximately four to seven inches long, depending on your bust size.

The first strip of tape is your lift strip. This is the most important strip, because it will determine how high your breasts look. You want to hold your breast up and position it where you want it. Place the tape at the base of your bust, under your apex. Press up, applying the tape vertically up your chest and over your nipple, extending it up your chest. Don't skimp on this strip of tape; you are going to trim it later, so make sure it is long enough and extends over your breast, reaching up for your collarbone. When you have taped both sides, it should look like the number eleven has been taped to your chest. Keep in mind that this is the lift strip, so you want to make sure your boobies are where you want 'em and that they are even!

The next strips will build your cleavage. You want to start under your bust, meeting the lift strip, and wrap the tape around the outside (armpit side) of your breast while pressing it closer to the center of your chest. The cleavage strips help hold your boobies up and in. Once you have done both sides, the four strips of tape should look like opposing half moons on your chest. The final tape strips should follow the shape of the first cleavage strip, working to cover more skin and press your bust closer together and toward the center of your body. These strips will fill in the half moon that was created by the lift strip and the cleavage strip.

Keep in mind that this tape should be the tough stuff: the extra-sticky, ain't-goin'-anywhere kind. The makers of duct tape have caught on to the need for alternatives to

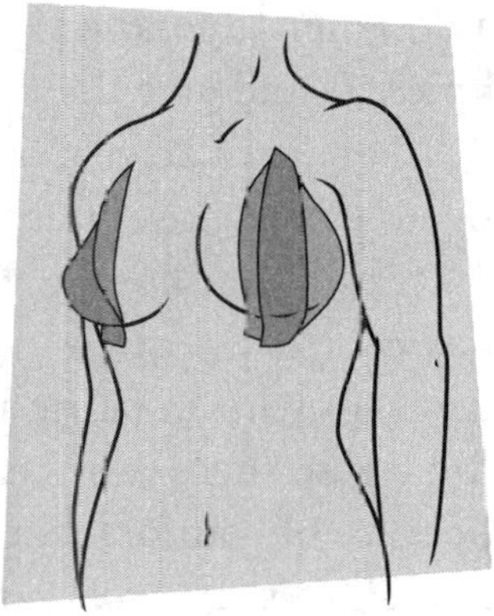

the traditional plumbing-pipe-silver version, and I am happy to report that you can find duct tape in every color of the rainbow. I keep a roll of duct tape in tan (nude) and one in black; these cover most of my tape-bra needs.

Once you've created your tape bra, it's time to slip into your outfit and trim the edges for a flawless look. Using small mustache scissors, gently pull the edges up and away from the body where needed. You need to be careful doing this, but trimming is an important part of the illusion. You don't want a tape edge to wave at your date while you are reaching for a hug or getting down on the dance floor.

When you're ready to remove your tape bra, hop in the shower and lather up. It will peel right off with some soap and water. If a shower isn't an option—you're too tipsy or tired—baby oil, or any oil for that matter, will help peel it off. Whatever you do, *never* pull off your tape bra without some form of lubricant to loosen the adhesive. This would be considered the booby equivalent of a Brazilian—'nuff said!

SUCK IT IN: SHAPEWEAR AND CONTROL GARMENTS

Now that we've mastered the bra, it's time to talk shapewear. Just as a better bra can make your bargain garments sing a designer tune, the right shapewear can smooth knockoff knickers and give them a pricey appearance.

There is an arsenal of modern girdles out there, just waiting to compact our flab into lovely feminine compartments. As traditional hosiery has fallen out of vogue, shapewear has picked up where control-top panty hose left off. The developments in fabric and construction have been extraordinary, so there is no reason to avoid these miracle workers because of comfort issues. I can honestly say that I find my bike short shapewear far more comfy than any bikini panty I have ever put on, and they give me the confident strut of an aerobics instructor. There are, however, a few details to look for when shopping for shapewear that will ensure a better, less sausage-like fit.

Shopping for Shapewear

Comfy shapewear can be found in the hosiery aisle of your local drugstore. I've found that whether you pay thirty dollars for a department store shaper or seven bucks at a drugstore, you can find the same level of control and comfort. Also, most of the high-end shapers are made at the exact same manufacturing facilities as the cheaper versions, so quite often you are getting the same thing for less than half of the price. And there is nothing better than making a pit stop at your favorite drugstore for a quick pint of ice cream and then heading right over to the hosiery aisle to add a guilt-free "hide and go slimmer" to your purchase. (Hee-hee!)

Just like the undesirable uniboob, you want to avoid unibuns, also known as barrel bottom. You need to look for a slimmer that lifts and separates your tushy just like your

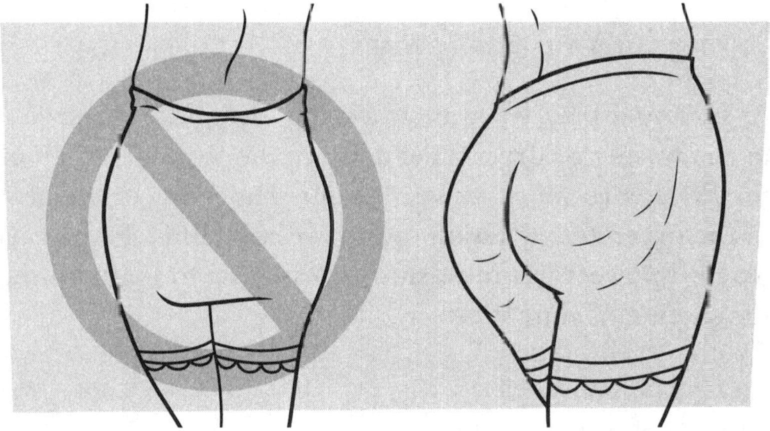

bust. Slimmers with a gathered center seam that fits nicely in your buttocks usually offer the best two-bun look.

From both a budget and a comfort standpoint, the bike short or capri style slimmers offer the best bang for the buck. The slip or skirt style shapewear can be worn only with skirts or dresses, and they tend to ride up and noticeably bind at the top of the knee (eew!); they also give you unibuns. No matter your preferred style, you want to make sure that the elastic at the leg and the waistband grips without cutting into you. Look for wider leg bands made of microfiber and elastin that won't create a prominent starting point of control. There is nothing worse than revealing the illusion of a fabulous shape with the visual ripple of bound abundance.

High-waisted slimmers that reach up and meet your bra band are also a great shape solution. The best ones have a thin ribbon of silicone sewn into the band so that it grips your rib cage and can't roll down into your waist. Never buy a slimmer without first inspecting the waistband and leg bands for smooth, invisible support.

Caring for Your Shapewear

As with your bras, you want to avoid putting your shapewear in the washer or dryer. Like dousing the Wicked Witch of the West with water, exposing your shapewear to the heat of the dryer and agitation of the washer will melt away its magical powers. Hand washing is essential to maintaining the suction of your slimmer.

HOSIERY

Traditional hosiery has been fading from women's wardrobes like the micromini. But whether or not you like the nylon leg chambers, hosiery can make or break your outfit. A bad hosiery choice can make your ensemble look less than sophisticated, and the right hosiery can give you a total style boost. The golden rule of hosiery is: If we can see your toes, we *should not* see your hose! There is no bigger hosiery sin than stocking feet in open-toed shoes.

When it comes to traditional hosiery, remember that beautiful legs and feet are an asset, and current fashion and etiquette demand that you show them off. Hosiery per se—aside from tights or fishnets—has not been seen on fashion runways for years. Hosiery rules still sadly apply to some of the corporate world, but the appearance of lovely legs and a beautiful pedicure framed by strappy sandals or open-toed shoes is more than OK in most situations—it's gorgeous!

If you have to wear hosiery, choose sheer, neutral shades that match your skin tone. Suntan hosiery looks obvious and tacky. I mean, who would believe that you vacationed in Saint-Tropez in a turtleneck while your legs soaked in the rays?

Creative Options for Your Legs

When it comes to winter tights or heavier hosiery, it's best to keep your color choices matched to your skirts or trousers. The unbroken line of a black skirt with black hosiery and black heels will always make you look taller and slimmer and will visually add sophistication and implied value to your outfit. This applies to any dark color, such as black, gray, brown, or navy. Interrupting the continual color flow with light-colored hosiery—even when you are just wearing pants or trousers—segments your legs and makes them appear shorter. If you are wearing a printed skirt or trousers, opt for tights that coordinate or match the darkest shade in the print, and then match the tights with dark-colored shoes.

My favorite hosiery magic is cast in the form of a thin nude fishnet. This subtle option doesn't scream "naughty"; it sends a confident, stylish message that adds visual interest and a little intrigue to your outfit. Nude fishnets are guaranteed to look modern and offer a stylish flair that will hype your ensemble as runway hot and worth a lot! You

STRIPED and loud-patterned tights pull focus to your feet and make your legs look stumpy. Pippi Longstocking owns this look—let her have it!

are sure to snag these holey hose for under ten bucks, and they'll pump up the perceived price tag of your entire look in seconds flat. (Woo-hoo!)

Airbrushed Leg Makeup

One of the best inventions since hair dye is spray-on leg makeup. You have to try this amazing leg shellac. These pantyhose in a can will diminish the appearance of veins, cuts, bruises, and other discolorations, leaving a soft, even-toned look. As in the case of regular hosiery, there is a high-end version that you can find at department stores, and there are great drugstore options that will work just as well. You can find specific suggestions at centsofstyle.com.

You will happily find that today's leg makeup won't sweat off on the dance floor, rub off on your party duds, or come off at the beach or pool without soap. For best results, spray it in your hands and apply it to your legs; don't spray directly on your legs. You should choose your shade the same way you would a foundation: try to match your skin tone perfectly. One spray can will last for several applications, so at an average price of under twelve bucks, it is much cheaper than panty hose. (Yippee!)

PANTIES

Panties—what a funny word. Whether you like full coverage, low-rise, boy shorts, high-cut briefs, string bikinis, or tanga thongs, your underwear affects your outerwear. Choosing the most comfortable and invisible panties should be your major goal for undies, and once you have found them, then you can focus on the other bottom line.

Saving S$ on Undies

Bargain panties are not always a bargain. If they bunch up, ride up, and mess up the look of your clothes, those two-dollar drawers have just cost you a bundle in fashion fabulousness. Once you find the breathable, untroubled fit of great undies, you want to go ahead and make the financial move to fill your lingerie drawer with seven pairs (five nude and two black). These will match your bras and have you feeling more confident no matter what you put on—and that is worth every cent.

If they are ridiculously expensive, then buy one or two pairs and search for better prices on shop.com or amazon.com. Both of these websites are designed to scan the Internet for the best price on your desired goods. You can additionally employ the bargain-bra hunt strategy and keep the style number of your favorite new panties programmed into your cell phone so that you can shop closeout and discount stores for thrifty-chic prices. It just doesn't get sweeter than unexpectedly finding your exact favorite items for pennies on the dollar at a closeout store.

Fabrics

The size and shape of your tummy, thighs, and tushy affect how your panties fit and ultimately whether your panties are going to stay put. The evolution of microfiber and advances in elastin, Lycra, and spandex have made a variety of undie styles more wearable for all shapes and sizes. Microfiber and mesh panties gently hug the skin and stay put so that they don't reach for the moon. Microfiber breathes, stretches, and holds its shape much better than all-cotton; so have no fear, blended fabrics are friendly fabrics that you want to include in your panty hunt.

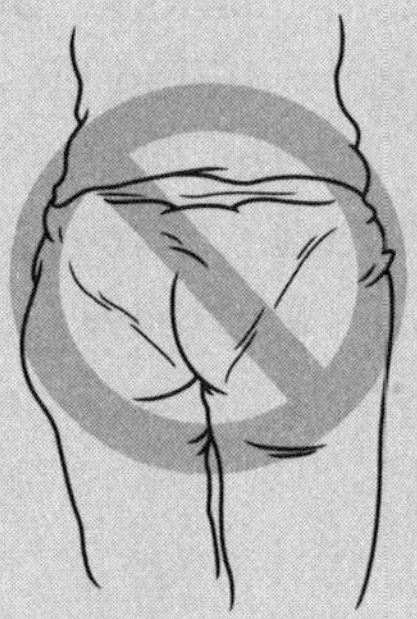

VPL (visible panty lines) is a fashion fatality. If you hate thongs and refuse to go commando, try alternative shapewear or foundation garments. Whatever you do, make sure you check your rear view before heading out the door.

Panty Style

One of the biggest panty discoveries of the past decade has been that snug elastic not only causes VPL, it causes cellulite. Yeah, that's right: the elastic in your panties may very well be causing the orange peel effect on your buns. It seems that snug, binding elastic causes the fat cells to bunch up and gather at the constriction point, which means they make you look bad with your clothes on and with your clothes off. This discovery has led to the development of "raw edge" panties, which hug the skin without an elastic piping.

There is no doubt that the technology and design development behind today's covered behinds are great, but in my opinion, your best bet will always be the thong. If you hate the thought of thongs, stop thinking about it, and just do it. I mean, if most of your panties are firmly intent on riding up your cheeks, you might as well find a comfy undie alternative that takes a shortcut to the party.

I have successfully converted my mother and my *grandmother* to the comfortable wonders of the perfect-fitting thong. If you have tried them and you hate them, you have not found the right thong for you and your body. Just like other panties, thongs come in many shapes and sizes, and you have to experiment a little to find a great fit.

Panty Fit

Great fit is what great underwear is all about. You have to *try them on*! Plan on wearing the smallest undies you currently own, and try on an assortment of panties over them to see how they fit and feel. You want to make certain your panties are working to create a smooth bottom and tummy, not pinch or create cinched areas of flesh that will ripple under your clothes. I know that this can be uncomfortable, but this small investment of time will save you cents in the long run. We all have a drawer full of panty mistakes. These panties rarely see the outside of our drawer, but we hang onto them because we spent the money and ya never know when you might have to have them.

Just remember that the goal of foundation garments is to create a fabulous, smooth, feminine silhouette that allows you to dress effortlessly and, most important, cost-effectively. The better your undies, the more you can look like a million without spending a fortune. *(Wink!)*

3 Does This Look Good on Me?

The Cuts, Fits, and Styles That Wow Every Woman's Shape

Once you have your undies in order, it is time to talk about fit. We are now in our third generation of women who either do not know how to or don't have time to sew. As an unfortunate result, many women are at a complete loss when it comes to knowing how to fit their body and what looks best on them. Garment construction, proportion, and visual balance are principles of sewing and design that are not being taught or handed down. High school home ec, the family sewing machine, and creative free time are disappearing like eight-track tapes, so dames don't have the tools or skills to recognize what shapes and styles will help build a better body.

Most of us are now at the total mercy of designers and store buyers, whose number one goal is to generate fresh new merchandise to feed the retail machine. The need for *new* quite often supersedes the goal of optimizing a woman's figure, as designers crank out ill-inspired shapes and silhouettes that don't always look great on the average woman. But in designers' defense, those of us who are slaves to fashion and comfort stuff our closets with a never-ending stream of clothes that should never have been made for a woman, much less bought and worn by one.

As consumers, we are bombarded with new styles and trends each season, all subliminally encouraging us to buy something new so we'll look refreshed and feel better about ourselves. Before ya know it, everyone is wearing the latest trend, and worse, it is all you can find in your local stores. So when we are surrounded by certain styles, no matter how hideous they look on us, it is easy to rationalize what's available as being "what's in style." I mean, who didn't have a pair of stirrup pants in her closet a few years back? I ask you, did these look good on us, or did they make us look like snow cone fashion stooges?

In addition to having lost the discipline of selecting a flattering fit, many of us have issues with our size. In a recent poll of women who visit my website, centsofstyle.com, 63 percent said they wear a dress size of 12 or larger, but only 37 percent said they feel this size range is perfect. The majority, 51 percent, said a size 8 or 10 is the perfect dress size. You can easily surmise that most of us are not happy with our size and want to look taller, slimmer, more shapely, and/or more feminine.

So lovely ladies everywhere want to look better and of course spend less money but are fumbling their way through shopping and dressing without the know-how to pull it off. Major moola is being wasted on fashion choices that ain't working! I mean, finding great bargains is only one element of the thrifty-diva equation. You need to know how to find clothes and dress your body in a way that celebrates your shape and optimizes your powerful femininity; that is what great fit is all about.

Before we dive into an enlightening pool of clothing fit principles, I want to be very clear that there is *no perfect size.* And for that matter, we should never hang our hat on the number that's stitched in our britches. There's so much designer delusion, vanity sizing, and budget sizing in the fashion industry that a standard sizing chart really doesn't even exist. We'll talk much more about this in the following chapters, but for now, know that the economic variables that go into determining whether a garment will be cut more sparingly or generously are so great that wrapping your ego around this number is emotional suicide—so don't do it!

Instead, select whatever size looks best on you. This may mean that you need to go up or down two to three sizes in some things to get the right fit. Choose the size that flows nicely from the fullest parts of you without binding or pulling, and without exception, work to create an hourglass shape through the waist.

If your clothes fit you beautifully, create visual balance, and offer feminine shape, you will always look amazing, no matter the size. So rock the figure you have, Hot Stuff—and don't sweat the digits!

FIT PRINCIPLES

In working with ladies of all shapes, sizes, and shades, I've learned that a few fit principles and guidelines are simply standard. A basic fit formula can be applied to every woman and will render the intended result of a stronger, more womanly shape. I've had the great pleasure of helping ladies who are as small as a girl's size 12 to ladies as fabulously full figured as a size 36, from four foot eleven to six foot three, and all of them revolutionized their image by applying these directives.

Of course, there are specific style tricks to help visually improve particular figure issues, but for the most part, classic design, garment construction, and fit elements are universally timeless and will enhance any figure. It is the details of the fit that make you look taller, thinner, and/or more shapely, and here is what to look for.

Pants

When it comes to the cut and fit of your trousers, jeans, cropped pants, and shorts, look for these fit and design elements:

- Pants and all legged bottoms should be comfortably fit to your hips and seat. Have them taken in to fit your waist or shortened if needed. If pants are too small and pull across this lower hip area, you'll get crotch whiskering or smiling, which only makes you look larger.

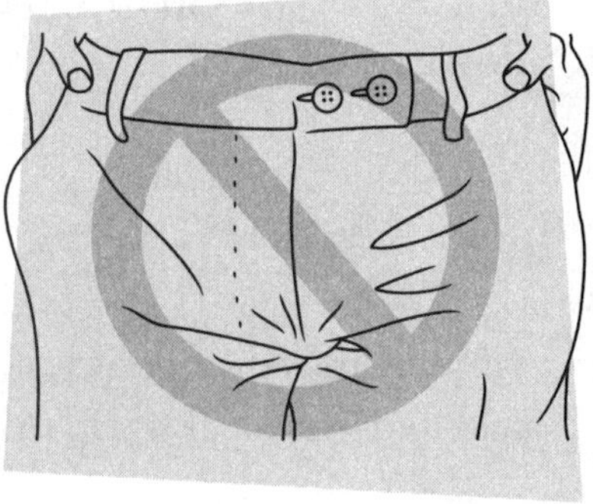

- Watch the rise. A rise that is too long and comes too far up on your waist tends to collapse in the front and create a masculine-looking crotch tent.

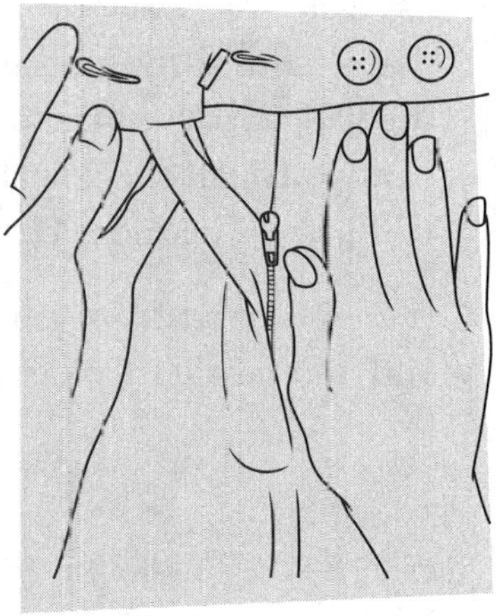

Longer rises also put a tummy pooch on display. A rise that hits around the belly button is best. A shorter zipper length is often an indicator of the rise. My rule is no zippers longer than your hand.

• On casual pants and jeans, get a better fit at the waist by opting for wider waistbands and larger yokes. (Yokes are the fitted parts of your pants that go around your waist; see "Denim Chic" in Chapter 5 for more info.) These allow the pants to sit closer to your hips and waist, creating a more flattering fit.

• Have pants hemmed to the base of the back of your foot when barefoot or to the base of the heel of your shoe to make your legs look longer. When hems hit around the ankle, they stunt the line of the leg and make you appear shorter. Remember, cuffs will also make you look shorter.

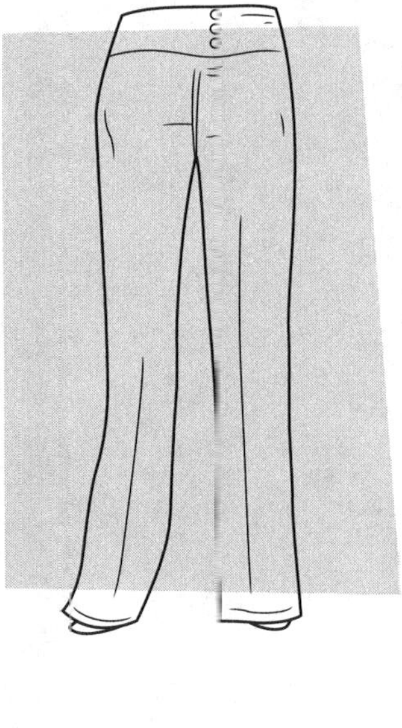

• Choose boot-cut, wide-leg, or straight-leg pants for visual balance. Stay away from a tapered-leg pant or anything too skinny; they will always make your butt look bigger!

Skinny pants can be tricky. As the widths of pant legs fluctuate with the seasons, I want you to be armed with the knowledge of how to tastefully navigate this dangerous image terrain. Choose a *straight leg* that is slim through the thigh and falls straight down from the fullest part of the hip. A straight leg will have the same slim width all the way down the leg to the bottom hem and will always be more flattering than a tapered leg.

- Choose flat-front pants without pleats. Pleats create girth and add fabric in areas where ya don't need it!

LYCRA, SPANDEX, OR ELASTIN—*stretch*—is added to many of today's trousers to help achieve a more feminine, body-conscious fit. One thing to remember when buying your new favorite, fits-me-like-a-glove britches is to note the amount of stretch in the fabric content. The higher the percentage of stretch, the more the trousers will grow or stretch out.

With every 1 percent of stretch content in your trousers, they will grow an overall average of 5 percent. So, a 4 percent elastic content can see your pants grow 20 percent overall, or nearly an entire size after just one wearing! Now, your pants will shrink back down after washing/cleaning, but a good rule of thumb when purchasing trousers with a higher level of stretch is to choose a *slightly* snug fit. Natural wear will help mold them to your body and achieve a comfortable give.

If the pants have a smaller percentage of stretch content, then pay closer attention to the comfort level and fit while in the dressing room. They are sure to grow a bit but will remain truer to size.

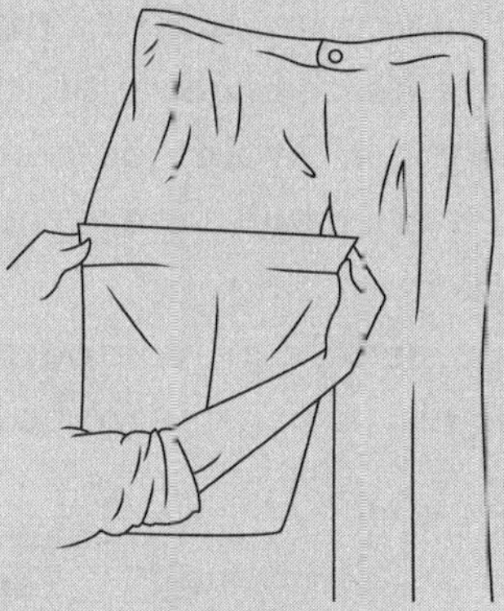

A QUICK way to check whether pant legs are straight or tapered is to bring the hem of one pant leg up to the base of the crotch. If the width of the hem and the width of leg at the seat or crotch area are the same, the pants are straight legged and will fall straight from the fullest part of your hip. If the hem width falls short of the leg width at the seat, the legs are tapered and will make your hips look larger.

- Stay away from side-zip pants with no detail. These can unnecessarily square your bottom and exaggerate the slightest tummy pooch.

- Avoid patterned trousers, cropped pants, or shorts. As a general rule, they are a recipe for disaster.

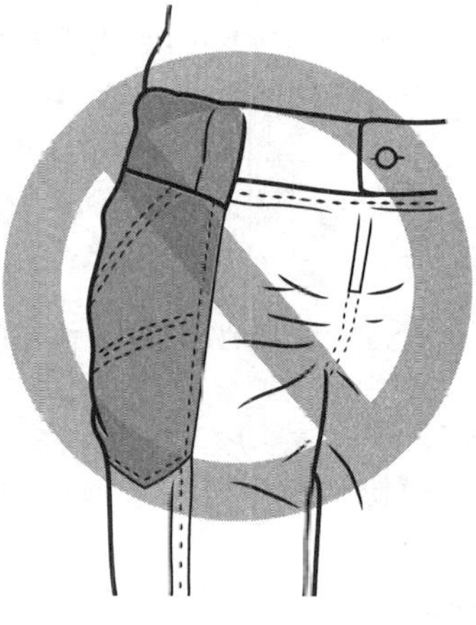

- Avoid front patch pockets on any of your trousers, cropped pants, or shorts. Patch pockets are little sewn-on fabric squares that square the area they are sewn on. When it comes to clothing details, you always want angles, contours, and curves—no squares.

• Check the placement of front and back pockets. Front pockets should be angled, reaching in and up toward a tiny waist. This visually draws the eye into the center of the body and creates a smaller-looking waist. Avoid side-seam or vertical pockets; they tend to splay open and square your hips and middle. Slanted front pockets are best.

Back pockets that sit low, angle up slightly, are contoured (not square), and hit in the middle of your tushy are best. Avoid pockets that sit high on the hip, anything square, and anything too small. The smaller the pocket, the bigger your bottom looks. Also, if "baby got back," avoid back pocket flaps. These create a visual butt-shelf that draws attention to an area you are looking to minimize.

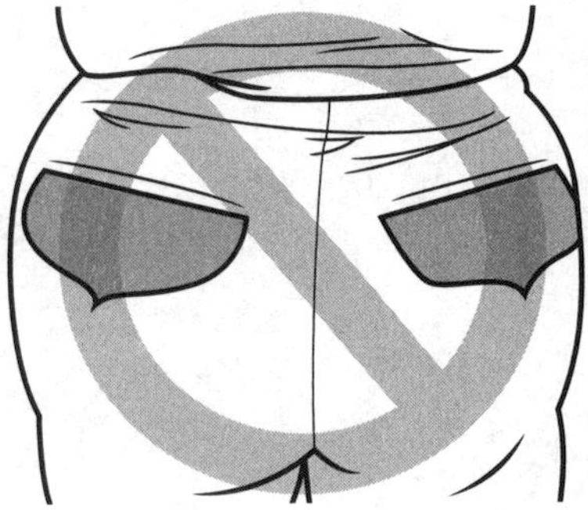

• Choose cropped pants, not capris, that hit just below the fullest part of your calf, approximately seven to nine inches off the floor. (Capris are tapered; cropped pants have straight legs.)

• Choose longer, darker trousers and jeans with little or no treatment. These make you look slimmer, taller, and more current. We will discuss finding your perfect jeans in Chapter 5. (Woo-hoo!)

Skirts and Dresses

When considering skirts and dresses, look for these visual fit cues:

- Make sure the fabric flows and hangs nicely from the fullest part of your hips and doesn't cup under them or pull across them. Fabric pulls across the hips create horizontal lines that highlight the size of your hips . . . no, thanks!

- Have skirts and dresses hemmed to the knee area. This length looks the most flattering on almost all women. A knee length introduces the curve of the calf and makes your legs look longer and more shapely.

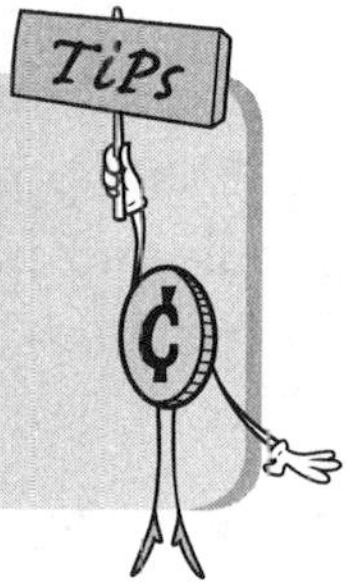

IF YOU do not have shapely legs, skirts cut just below the fullest part of the calf and paired with a slim, high-heeled shoe will offer a leaner-looking, shapely leg. (Insert wolf whistle here.)

- Straight skirts, fluted skirts that kick out at the knee, and A-line skirts that lie flat across the tummy are all flattering styles on most figures. Pleated or gathered skirts should release at the low hip or around the seat. Extra fabric should not be gathered at the waist or tummy.

- Skirts and dresses with medium-sized to large patterns can camouflage a tummy, but remember that the smaller the pattern, the larger you will look, so choose prints wisely. Avoid horizontal details of *any* kind at all cost.

THE NUMBER one most flattering skirt style on every body type is an A-line skirt cut to the knee. If you are petite, you should wear skirts just above the knee; if you are taller, you can wear them at the base of the knee. No matter your size, A-line skirts create an hourglass shape by emphasizing a smaller waist and diminishing your badonka-donk.

Jackets, Cardigans, and Second Layers

Jackets, cardigans, and second layers in general are very important garments. These are your style makers, the fabulous toppers that instantly pull a look together, adding polish and panache. The fit of these pieces is very important because they help build structure and feminine shape. Follow these guidelines to find a fabu fit:

- Make sure your jacket or blazer hem ends around your hip bone or extends no more than four inches (four fingers) below your hip bone. Longer jackets that hit around the seat area always look more masculine, make your legs look shorter, and create a widening line right at the fullest part of your body—*not good!*

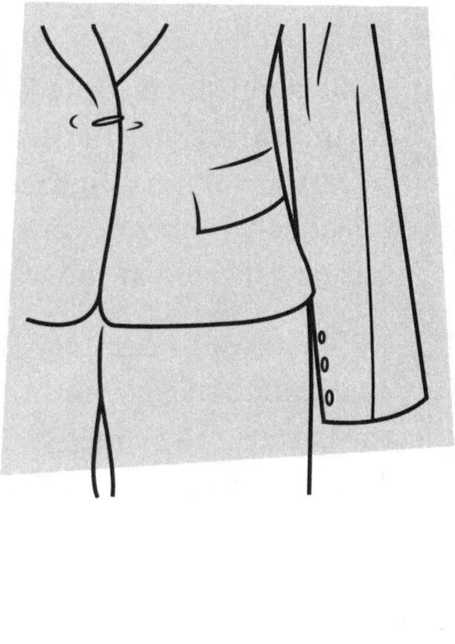

TIPS

AN EASY way to tell where a jacket is going to hit you without even trying it on is to look at the sleeve length. If the hem of the jacket ends above the hem of the sleeve, it will offer a shorter, more feminine, flattering fit. If the hem extends past the sleeve length, you know it will be too long and a visual no-no.

- When you first try on a jacket, blazer, or any top layer, reach for your waist button or cinching waist detail. If there is a center button that hits you at the smallest part of your waist, then all of the other seams will lie properly.

If this detail is off, hitting above or below the smallest part of you, the entire garment will collapse around your middle, causing pulls and folds of fabric at the bust. Additionally, all of the figure-enhancing seams will be off, ruining the intended effect. Your waist button is a major fit indicator. If it's off, everything else will be, too.

- Be careful with shoulder pads. Both shoulder pads and shoulder seams should end at the edge of your shoulder for better balance and structure. No drop shoulders! They make you look slope-shouldered and dowdy.

• Check armholes to make sure they fit close to the underarm and are not oversized. Oversized armholes affect the fit of the bust and waist. You want them to fit comfortably under the arm but not hang too low.

• Jacket pockets are best when angled and slanted up toward the center of your body. Avoid squares and straight lines whenever possible.

• The sleeve length of your jackets should end between the top of your wrist and your first thumb knuckle. Any longer, and the sleeves need to be shortened.

• Choose V-neck cardigan sweaters and second layers; button these under the bust to create shape. Avoid crewneck or round-neck cardigans for the most figure-flattering fit.

Shirts, Blouses, and Tees

Your shirts, blouses, and tees reflect your shape and creativity in a significant way. As with all of your garments, the fit through the waist is very important. If your tops square your shape, you have lost your visual feminine fashion power. Make sure to follow these guidelines for the most impactful fit:

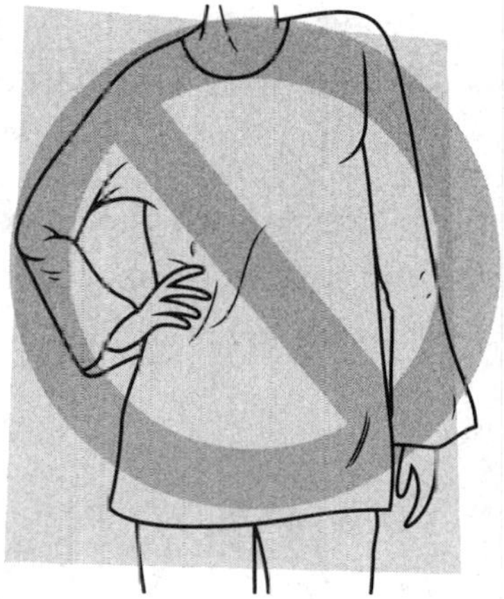

• All of your tops *must* either have darts or seaming or else have Lycra, spandex, or elastin so that they can skim the body and offer a womanly shape. Avoid any top that does not help create or enhance your hourglass.

• All women look best when they showcase their décolletage. An open neckline broadens the shoulders and balances the hips. Additionally, the higher the neckline, the lower your boobies look. V-neck, scoopneck, and off-the-shoulder tops are universally flattering. Avoid round collars and crewneck tops and T-shirts; they lower your bust and look manly.

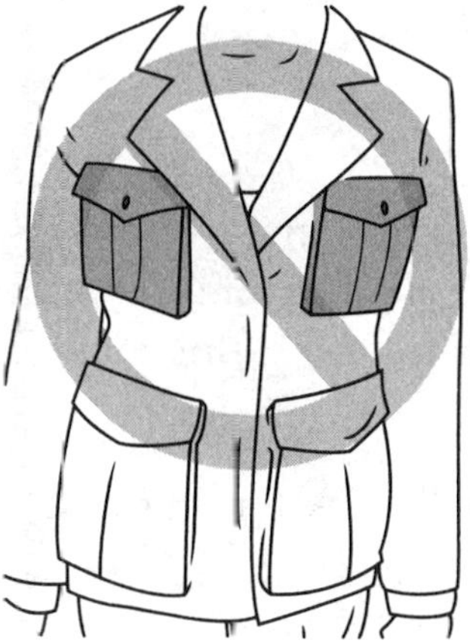

• Avoid big square booby pockets on your tops! You always want angles, contours, and curves—no squares. Smaller breast pockets are better, but *no* breast pockets are best.

• Check the button placement on your shirts and blouses. Make sure there is an apex button (button parallel with your nipples) for the best fit. Buttons that hit above and below the fullest part of your bust line always splay open. Avoid man shirts with button-down collars—way too masculine. (Remember, they must have seaming, darts, Lycra, spandex, or elastin.)

• Check both the apex seam and the bust seam on all of your tops for proper placement. (Apex seams should point to your nipple, and bust seams should be *under* the breast.)

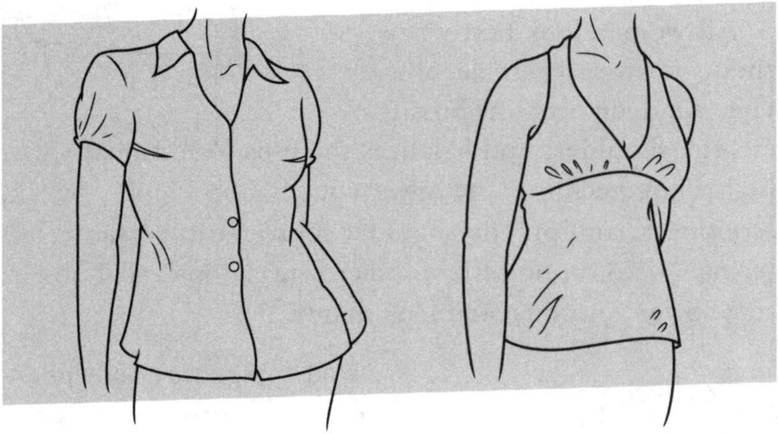

• Two nice, feminine short-sleeved options are short flutter sleeves and cap sleeves cut at a slant. Avoid sleeves cut straight across the fullest part of the arm; this looks matronly.

• Avoid horizontal stripes of any kind. Look for diagonal stripes instead.

• If you layer your tops, make sure you have fitted under pieces, and keep in mind that the lightest pieces should be worn closest to your body and build out in weight.

NO NEED to give your favorite (figure-flattering) fuzzy sweater the cold shoulder. Just put it on ice! Place fuzzy winter items like scarves, hats, and sweaters that tend to shed in a large Ziploc bag, and put them in the freezer overnight. The next day, your unruly knits will be almost completely fuzz free. I'm not sure how it works, but it does!

I'M NOT PREGNANT! MINIMIZE YOUR MIDDLE

When I asked subscribers to my website, centsofstyle.com, to tell me their number one fashion camouflage issue, a whopping 61 percent admitted a problem with their pooch. Tummies are the overwhelming camouflage issue by far. The next closest issue was larger thighs, but only 13 percent claimed it was their camouflage priority. Since the paunch tends to be the major prob, here are a few tips to help minimize your middle:

- **Don't cover up!** Now, I know this sounds all wrong, but the truth is, if you completely hide your middle under shapeless tops and long jackets, you are only making the problem worse. You are giving the impression of "a bun in the oven."

- **Bisect the bulge.** The best way to strategically minimize your tummy is to actually have your clothing *bisect* the problem, not completely cover it. This means your trousers should not come all the way up over your tummy, and your tops should not go all the way down over it. They should overlap in the middle around your belly button. You need to choose trousers that divide the plane of your tummy and break up the area to deemphasize it. Zippers, slanted pockets, wider waistbands, and yokes all work to make an area look smaller.

- **Your waistband should smile.** You want your trousers, skirts, and jeans to have a midrise that smiles in the front, allowing the waistband to hit you around your bellybutton while your actual waistline remains captured at the sides.

- **Structure, seams, and spandex are your friends.** As explained before, *all* of your blouses, shirts, and other tops must have one of two things: a percentage of Lycra, spandex, or elastin, or else shape-creating darts and seams.

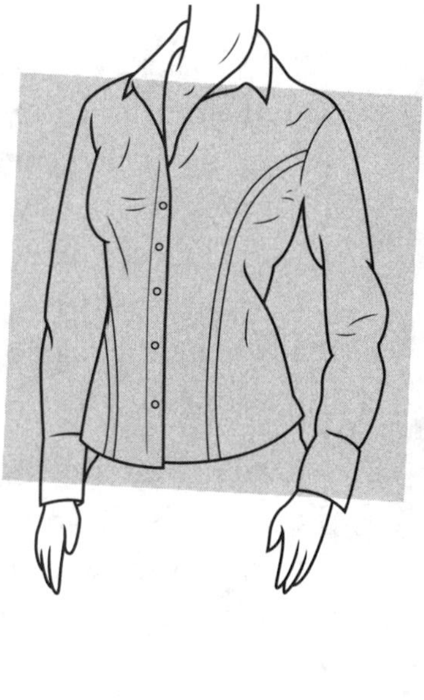

Loose, boxy, shapeless tops and jackets make your tummy look larger than it really is. You can create an hourglass shape by letting your clothes do all of the work. And remember, you want your tops and jackets to end around your hip bone.

- **Belts aren't bad.** You can wear belts, but you want to wear them *atop* untucked knits and under jackets. A belt peeking

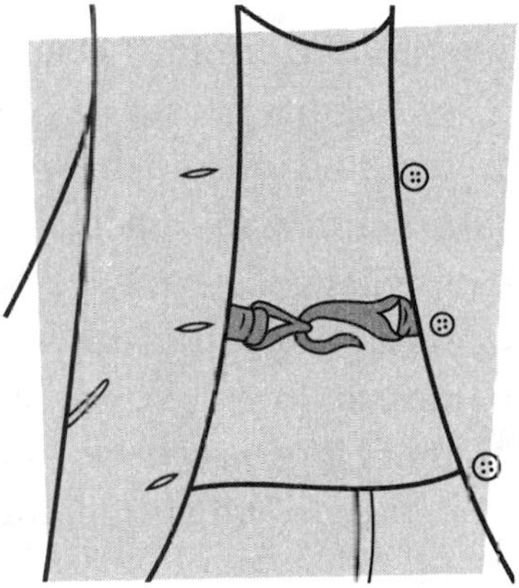

out from the opening of a jacket can be very slimming. The jacket prevents the eye from seeing the entire width of your waistline, and the belt bisects the tummy, making it look smaller.

However, if you are not wearing a jacket, this fashion trick *does not work!*

- **The bolder, the better.** Tiny, mousy prints make you look larger and highlight your bulges. Larger, colorful, graphic prints fool the eye and work to camouflage a tummy much better.

- **Ruche! Ruche! Ruche!** Ruching (chunky gathering of fabric) is another way to fool the eye into thinking you have fewer bumps and bulges. Well-placed ruching down the middle of a top or at the waistline of a dress is a modern fashion illusion, as you can't tell the difference between a roll of fabric and a roll of your own creating. *(Wink!)*

Remember, showcasing or creating a waistline is one of the most important and powerful fashion decisions you make every day. You can do it! Simply follow these steps, and you will be on your way to looking and feeling more feminine, no matter what size your middle.

SWIMSUIT SANITY

I know it's daunting, but you can absolutely find a fabulous swimsuit that builds confidence and has you ready to whoop it up in the sun. I decided to include a section on swimsuits because I get flooded with questions from desperate dames each April, wondering how to hide the sins of winter. *Everybody* has figure issues that she would like to change, so you are not alone. No matter what, don't let water fun opportunities go by because of swimsuit insecurities. Follow these tips, and you will happily find a swimsuit that helps you work your she-stuff.

Before you head out shopping, keep these things in mind:

- If you schedule—yes, schedule—the shopping trip on a weekday morning, you will have fewer eyes in the dressing room and more sales help to assist you.
- If you apply a self-tanner the night before, you will lessen the shock of a ghostly glow and be more apt to like what you see in the mirror.
- If you wear a thong or at least small bikini panties, you will get a better idea of what your swimsuit will look like, since you have to try it on over your undies.
- Don't go shopping with clunky shoes on! Shopping with sandals or flip-flops on will help you better visualize your smokin' hot self at the pool or beach.

Once you are at your favorite store, with nice salespeople, good lighting, and excellent prices (I pray!), remember this:

- Even if you think you know your size, plan to take your size and one size *larger* into the dressing room. Then try on the larger one first. With designer sizing being all over the board, you will feel much less deflated if you have to go down a size versus going up.

- Choose your style of suit the way you would choose your lingerie. If you know that your bust line requires an underwire bra for support, then you need to choose a bathing suit with an underwire. If your favorite foundation garments give you the shape that you like best, look for a suit with built-in support. And when it comes to selecting a bathing suit bottom, mimic the style of undies that you feel most confident in.

- Stay focused on the *good*. If you have gorgeous eyes, choose a suit that will pull focus to them; if you have beautiful skin, choose a color that will flatter it; if you have a great bust line, look for a suit that flatters "the girls"; if you have long legs, choose a suit that highlights the enviable length. Come on, we all have good stuff, so let's stay focused on that!

Now you are at the rack. Take a deep breath, but keep these tips in mind, based on your own body type:

- **Full bust:** Halter tops with thicker straps and underwire are best. This style will help capture the full breast and offer the best lift.

- **Small bust:** Molded form cups, cups with a pocket for a silicone insert, underwire cups, and front closures offer the best bust enhancement. Bright colors and bold patterns also work wonders.

- **Tummy control:** Choose a one-piece suit with a shaper panel built in for support.

- **Larger thighs:** Opt for a solid-color bottom and a bold, printed top. Choose a plunging top with thicker straps placed farther apart to create more visual balance. You can also choose a skirted bottom, but make sure that the side edges of the skirt smile or turn up to create a longer leg line. A skirt that goes straight across can highlight the size of the thighs.

When it comes to a cover-up, choose a beautiful wrap or bandeau that matches your suit bottoms and feels more glamorous. Avoid wearing oversized T-shirts, overalls, or men's swim trunks. You will have more confidence and look better if you have a swimming ensemble that you like.

- **Bumps and bulges:** Opt for larger prints and darker color combinations.

- **Boyish shape:** To create more shape, choose high-cut or French-cut legs on your bottoms and enhancing plunging halters.

- **Flat bottom:** Choose a suit with a lift panel to round out your shape à la J-Lo.

Set your intention to find a fabulous swimsuit that you love and that looks great on you, and don't stop until you do. Try on all types of suits that follow your body shape guidelines, in many colors and patterns, because swimsuits never have hanger appeal. You never know what enhancing properties a swimsuit has in store for you until you try it on. Good luck! I'll see you at the beach.

A FEMININE-FIT SHOPPING CHECKLIST

Looking great every day, whether you are headed to the office, the movies, or the pool, is a choice. As long as you make strategic, thrifty-chic, fashionable, well-fitting choices at the store, choosing to look fabulous every day is easy. When your closet is full of ill-fitting choices, you are bound to fall into a pattern of not looking your best. We all have the power to create the image of our dreams with the body we currently have. Don't make a purchase without referring to this simple feminine-fit checklist:

- Does this garment showcase my waist?
- Does this garment skim my body with ease, not too loose or too tight?
- Are the construction elements—buttons, pockets, zippers, seams and darts, hems, and so on—executed to create a flattering fit?
- Do my hips and seat look visually balanced by my shoulders and décolleté?
- Does this garment diminish my figure flaws and highlight my assets?

When your clothes fit you well and you look more shapely, you carry yourself with more confidence. Celebrate your womanly shape (smokin' hot bod) through your clothing, and revel in the fun of getting dressed and bein' a girl. Think of your clothes as an expression of your spirit, and don't be afraid to let it shine. Remember, there is nothing more comfortable than looking fabulous. *(Wink!)*

4

Uh, Don't Do That

We are all guilty of crimes of fashion. Jelly shoes, genie pants, and fringed headbands are just a few of the memorable mistakes that come to mind when I ponder the fashion atrocities of my past. My grandmother has a horrible photo of me that she pulls out every now and then to remind me, "You ain't so big for your britches." In it, I'm pridefully sporting the "Let's Get Physical" ensemble I wore nearly every weekend of 1981 to Rambo's Skateland in Saraland, Alabama. Neon-yellow pom-poms, glitter laces, and battery-powered skate lights are not captured by the photo, but you should know they were there!

The truth is, nobody wants to look like a fashion fool. No one wakes up, looks in her closet, and says, "Today I shall look like poo!" We all do the best we can and, for the most part, use our best judgment until we've been made aware of better options. I believe this theory wholeheartedly and have built my business on a platform of understanding, knowing it's my job to help inform and not to judge. I'm here to illuminate a brighter fashion path, not throw folks under the style bus for wearing bad britches.

That said, the national devotion to sloppy, comfortable clothes keeps me in an absolute tizzy and has become seriously ridiculous. At Any Mall USA on any given Saturday, you will find hundreds of women who have willingly sacrificed their power, femininity, and confidence by opting to drown in fabric, logos, and flip-flops. Shapeless, bulky body drapes hang on the masses, sucking any sign of style or feminine form like fashion vampires during an eclipse.

Worse, many of these comfortable style choices (term used loosely here) are rationalized as being such a great bargain "it just couldn't be passed up." I hear this all the time. Really, that three-dollar green plaid man shirt with honkin' booby pockets just couldn't be left at the store? Let me guess . . . it's comfortable!

For the record, just because it's on sale does not mean it's a bargain for you and your body. If a twenty-dollar pair of cropped pants squares your butt, makes your tummy pooch out and legs look stumpy, and has a pattern that might as well declare "wide load," what is this saving? These twenty-dollar gauchos are actually costing you . . . plenty! The golden nugget of frugal fashion fabulosity is knowing when things work for your body and when they *don't.*

There are several *Uh, Don't Do Thats* scattered throughout the chapters, and you will find a font of fashion faux pas at my website (centsofstyle.com). People are always commenting about how much they laugh at and love the *Uh, Don't Do Thats* on the site. But don't laugh so fast; go give a look and see if you too have fallen prey to a fashion flub. I've promised to help and not judge, but who says enlightenment can't be funny?

Though we are never at a loss for a style stumble, I wanted to dedicate a few pages to some fashion mishaps that live in many, if not most, closets. As I travel the country conducting Beauty Boot Camps in every state in the union, I've discovered that there is predictability to wardrobe mistakes, so let's get the wardrobe wreckers out of the closet. There are just some looks that should be outlawed. Steer clear of these fashion don'ts. Your friends and neighbors will thank you. And remember, there is nothing more comfortable than looking fabulous!

WEEKEND WEAR

- Helloooo . . . is there a beautiful woman under that baggy, shapeless, masculine fleece tent? Horrible oversized sweatshirts add forty pounds and smother any glimmer of feminine shape.

- Your weekend wear should excite and energize you to have fun, not to mention help you look fabulous. Choose colorful activewear that creates shape through the waist, ends around your hip bone, and contains Lycra or spandex.

It's just as easy to throw on a flattering active jacket as it is a fleece blob.

• Sweatpants with elastic bands at the bottom add bulk to your lower half and look like oversized clown bloomers. Try straight-leg yoga or running pants instead. You still get the simplicity of just pulling them on, but the cut and lighter-weight fabric create a much more figure-friendly look.

• Overalls make our "alls" look *huge.* We thought we were so cute in the nineties, sporting our high ponytails and legged denim sack with shoulder straps. Let's face it, we weren't cute! Overalls widen our middle, add bulk to our tummy, flatten our bottoms and our boobs, and make us look like dudes. If overalls are still your weekend wear, quit it!

SKIRTS

• If an ankle-length body tube is hanging in your closet, use it to insulate your water heater. Casual ankle-length skirts make us look like shapeless tree trunks. When I talk about owning your curves and celebrating your femininity, that includes showcasing your gams.

A knee-length A-line skirt that falls freely from the largest part of the hip is a timeless silhouette that is the most flattering on everyone, from your grandma to your cousin Gracie.

• Wearing rows and rows of horizontal details across your bottom is never a good idea, especially in a skirt. Whether they're from stripes, rickrack, ribbons, or ruffles, keep all wide lines and voluminous details off your rump. Details should work to visually slim, enhance, or create a better shape. Vertical or diagonal details elongate and can help build an hourglass. Keep the focus on your waist, not your posterior.

TROUSERS

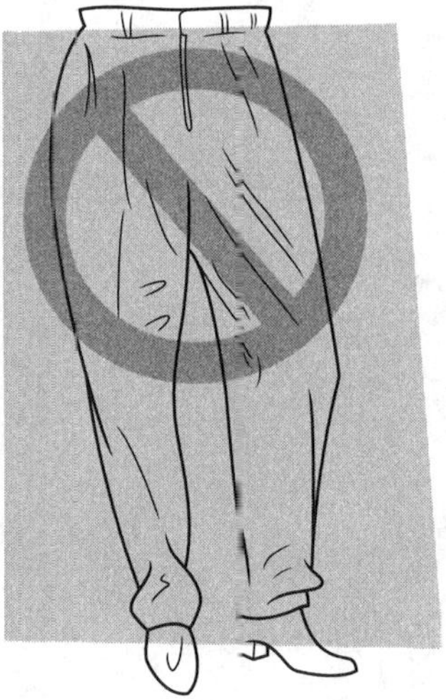

• As I mentioned in Chapter 3, tapered-leg pants and pleats are a huge fashion felony. Choose flat-front boot-cut or stovepipe-leg pants hemmed to the bottom of your heel to make your legs look longer and your hips look smaller.

• Tight low-rise jeans and/or pants, heavy belts, and tiny tees put your pooch on parade. This look also prohibits the gathering of any good-luck pennies (no bending over). Nobody wants to see the revealing introduction to your booty! This preposterous look has got to go! To keep your junk in your trunk and avoid a muffin top, choose pants with a comfortable waistband that frowns in the back and smiles in the front. This style trick will ensure that your natural waist and bottom are captured without adding to the length of the rise.

• Leggings should never be worn as pants. Consider leggings to be modern tights. They are to be layered under skirts and dresses, not worn to the grocery store with a cropped top and sneakers!

• Don't wear see-through white pants. The outline of the pockets through the pants looks really tacky. Choose white pants that are lined or made of a heavier fabric to ensure no pocket peekaboo.

• Bad denim treatment, including bleaching around the butt of your jeans, can be booty-vicious. Be sure to check your rear view before you leave the fitting room. Any "butt treatment" should be subtle and make your bottom look plump and peachy, not big and bleachy!

TOPS

• Stop wearing oversized shirts! Hiding under shapeless, oversized tops actually makes you look larger than you really are. No matter your size, a fitted blouse or top that has shape-enhancing seams, darts, and Lycra and/or spandex is a much better, feminine choice.

• Theme clothing is OK for children or a costume party, but

adults should steer clear of stacked doggie cardigans, Mickey Mouse jackets, Santa sweaters, and Halloween vests. These things just look frumpy and ridiculous. A great V-neck or scoopneck sweater in a vibrant, festive color is a much better choice. Be sure to choose a sweater that skims the body and offers shape and not bulk. Add a holiday accessory, like a beautiful brooch, for sophisticated style.

- Oh, baby, baby, midriff tops are done. Stick a fork in them, pull down your shirt, and ship back that useless Ab Master while you can still get a refund! Showcase your new belly ring at the beach, not a bar mitzvah. Figure-flattering tees and tops in saturated colors that skim the body and demurely reflect your shape are a much better bet.

- Thick, chunky, oversized, shapeless, floppy cable-knit sweaters are a fashion crime against your figure. Swollen, puffy winter sweaters could make Kate Moss look like the Michelin Man. Thinner, fine-gauge sweaters can offer the same amount of warmth when layered with a soft, body-conscious undershirt. The combo will give you a much more polished look.

THE BEST way to avoid the pesky stink-proof stripes of deodorant all over your shirt is to roll your shirt up from the bottom hem to the armholes. Slip it on, and then roll it back down. Your top will be white-stuff free . . . no sweat!

JACKETS

- If you have an acid-washed denim jacket, circa 1986, still hanging in your closet, it is time to let go! Please! Just let go! A fitted prewashed denim blazer that offers a feminine silhouette is a much better choice.

- The designer and fabric content label stitched to the sleeve of your winter coat is to be removed after purchase. This label was placed there for your shopping convenience. It is not intended to be an accessory or an enhancing detail!

SHOES

- Frankenstein's monster was big, green, and dim-witted in the movies; why would you want to wear his shoes? There is nothing feminine, modern, or attractive about thick, chunky man shoes. Plus, the thicker the sole, the thicker your legs look. A lighter, updated loafer with a kitten heel or contoured heel is both a modern and classic substitution.

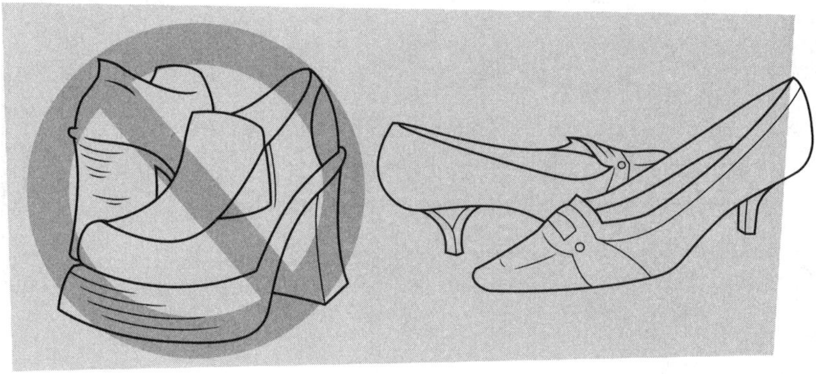

• Roman ankle straps wrapped high on the leg tend to rank high on the "hoochie" scale, not to mention make your legs look shorter. Keep your ankle straps wrapped close to your ankles for a much more flattering look.

• This is a tough one for me, because I know many ladies who engage in the frightening practice of wearing white pumps, often with suntan hosiery. *(Gulp!)* So here goes . . . White pumps are *evil.* They overpower everything you wear with them, pull focus to your feet, and almost always look cheap, cheap, cheap. Great silver pumps or slingbacks are a modern option that will look gorgeous with all of your summer whites and much more.

• For the record, if your tootsies hit the street, literally, your sandals don't fit. Toe overhang is T.A.C.K.Y.! Make sure your toes are neatly captured in your sandals. As a general rule, you want about a half inch (a pinky nail's worth) of room at the heel and toe of your sandal to ensure proper fit.

• OK, OK, OK, they are comfortable. But hulking sneakers are also the ugliest, bulky, he-man jock shoes in the world. How are you supposed to feel like a beautiful woman when you're lumbering about in styro-rubber-engineered foot buckets? Sleek, declunkified, urban walking shoes are a feminine option that doesn't make you look like you are ready for a pickup game at the park. You don't have to sacrifice style and femininity for comfort; modern options abound.

• Never, ever wear socks and sandals. This sloppy fashion flub tells the world you've given up. Come on, Hot Stuff, you know better! Socks should be captured in shoes, and sandals are for freshly painted toes.

YOU ARE WHAT YOU WEAR

There is no escaping it, what you wear says a lot about you. Your fashion choices reflect your self-respect, the occasion, and even your deference to the company you keep. What you put on has the power of a visual voice. Your clothes are a tool that can convey confidence, capacity, creativity, and charisma without a single spoken word. So considering the dynamic potential of clothing—something we all have to buy and wear anyway (most of us don't live in a nudist camp)—why would you choose to tell the world you'd rather be napping, as you sport a *comfortable* outfit that's barely a step above footie pajamas?

Smarter fashion choices simply make you look smarter. The better you dress your body, the better the initial perceptions of those you meet and come in contact with. And when you consider the cost-cutting strategies you will now be employing, you are gonna look bloody brilliant!

5 Closet Evaluation and Organization

CLEANING OUT YOUR closet is always tough, because our clothes hold memories and ignite feelings and emotions. We all remember the dress we wore for a special date with our honey or the business suit that got us our first *real* job or the jeans that made us feel like a rock star. Letting go of garments that we don't wear anymore but still have fondness for can often be bittersweet.

Many of us avoid cleaning out our closet to avoid the guilt. For some crazy reason, we haven't been able to lose the ten or so pounds that would have us dancing in the streets in our old duds, and cleaning out the closet means facing our weight issues. We think, "I know I will be a size 8 again, and I will be able to wear that." Truth is, when you lose the weight, the first thing you want is new clothes. The last thing you want to do is put on something decades old to celebrate your new body. You want new party frocks and sexy modern look-at-me wear, not parachute pants and a dress from the Alexis Carrington Collection circa 1984.

And did I mention money spent on clothes that we simply can't or never will wear again is another source of guilt? But it's not just the money; it's facing the bad decisions, the passing of time and getting older, our changing body and new priorities. Cleaning out your closet is hard, because quite often, what it really means is admitting we were wrong.

Many closets are full of the same mistakes made over and over again. We tend to consistently buy similar versions of the same garment, thinking that a certain style or cut is best for us. We get stuck in an image rut, continually striving to re-create an outfit or a look that represents a time in our life when we felt the most beautiful, the most successful, the most loved and celebrated. We shop to fill our closet with clothes that will ignite those warm, fuzzy feelings when we look in the mirror. As a result, we have a closet full of the same stuff in twenty different colors. When we are tipped to the fact that all of it looks heinous on us, we are hardly quick to succumb.

With all of this emotional attachment, separation anxiety is understandable. This is why the average woman actually wears less than 20 percent of her closet's contents on a regular basis. We live with the delusion that we have a much larger wardrobe than we really do. We all stand in front of our closet that's slap full of clothes and declare that we have nothing to wear. Damn that Eve. If she had not eaten that darn apple, then we would be happy as jaybirds, running naked and free.

Of course, it's not true that we have nothing to wear; it's that we have nothing to wear that fits well and optimizes our figure. Nothing that makes us feel empowered, feminine, and stylish. Nothing that projects our inner fashionista or that will render passers-by awestruck at our subtle creativity and unique flair. Now, that is what we really mean when we say we have nothing to wear!

So it is time to look at your closet in a whole new way. It's time to let some things go, figure out what you are doing wrong, and whittle your wardrobe down to what really works for you and your body. Don't be scared. I will help you, and you may be surprised to find that you have more style options hanging in your closet than you think.

DONATE, RE-CREATE, CONTEMPLATE, FITS ME GREAT

Before we get started, you might want to revisit the fit principles laid out in Chapter 3. Understanding the fit guidelines that will make your body look the most lean, feminine, and shapely, as well as the tailoring and garment construction issues that make a garment look more expensive, is key to a successful wardrobe weeding. And just like everything in life, once you understand and know how, it's easy.

As you are going through your closet and trying things on, I want you to apply the fit principles I've suggested in Chapter 3. For example, look for good button placement; remember, poor button placement can throw off the whole fit. Check for balanced lapels and for pocket size and placement. Make sure your bust and apex seams hit at the right places, and check for well-placed darts. Make sure your sleeve length is good, your skirts are the most flattering length, and your trousers work with your shape. Check the zippers and the side seams to make sure that they lie flat and patterns match up. The fit and the construction details are what make your budget garments look like a million bucks. (I'll explain more in Chapter 6.)

It's time to fearlessly approach your closet for a major purge. I propose that you clear a space for four clothing piles: you will need room for a Donate pile, a Re-Create pile, a Contemplate pile, and a Fits Me Great pile. If you'd like to use laundry baskets and/or make little signs so you don't get confused as the clothes are flying, please feel free. Containers and signs will certainly make the process seem more official, which is a good thing.

Your Donate pile will be for those hopeless garments that should no longer be in your wardrobe. These "never again" items such as tapered elastic-waist pants, oversized shapeless sweatshirts, holiday vests with big poofy appliqués, and overalls of any kind, just to name a few monstrosities, need to be retired. Your Donate garments are those "Uh, Don't Do That" (Chapter 4) items that are either worn out or too unflattering and awful to be worn out—out in public, that is!

Though these items are no longer of use to you, they may offer help and comfort to others in need locally or around the world, so you don't want to just throw them away. The Salvation Army, Goodwill, St. Vincent de Paul, and many other charities are always happy to receive your old clothes for distribution to the less fortunate. Let this be your solace as you say so long to your neon-blue Lycra leopard hot pants.

Your Re-Create pile is the most important one. This pile represents all of your wardrobe "capital." This stack of hopefuls is going to help you re-create your *shmaashing* Cents of Style wardrobe. This collection will include the garments that can find new life with just a couple of inexpensive alterations and the garments in good condition that can be placed on consignment at your favorite local consignment shop.

Now that you know what makes a garment right for you, you can determine what, if any, alterations will make an *almost* garment look great on you. Minor, inexpensive adjustments can change a "hate it" garment to a "yippee, I love it" garment in no time. These garments are potential diamonds in the rough, and this is a great way to optimize what you already have. You liked it enough to buy it in the first place; you might as well get some use out of it, right? But if this alteration will cost more than twenty bucks, I would give it some serious thought. If you hold true to the Cents of Style budget-shopping principles, you can probably replace the garment for under fifty dollars, so weigh the options carefully.

The goal here is to spend a little money to make your underutilized garments more functional. These alterations will, of course, make the clothes look more tailored, which will in turn make them look richer—delightfully thrifty chic! A great tailor can make you look ten pounds lighter—yippee!

For example, you could shorten a jacket and/or take it in at the waist for a much more flattering fit. You could add darts to that beautiful boxy blouse to give it a more modern, fitted look. How about creating cropped pants from trousers that the dry cleaner shrank, or shortening that skirt so that it makes your legs look longer and shapelier? You could also have a more flattering neckline cut into an underused top or have pleats taken out of pants for a more flattering fit. I want you to focus on the potential of the garments that you don't wear; if nothing else, this will make you a better shopper.

Your Re-Create pile will also be for those garments that would be too costly to alter but are worth placing on consignment. A visit to your tailor will probably help you decide which option is best. Keep in mind (as explained in Chapter 6) that most consignment stores will take only freshly cleaned items *in season*. But at a 40 to 50 percent return on the sale price, this is a great way to generate new wardrobe cash. You could even use your consignment store credit to do some thrifty-diva shopping of your own. In fact, shopping with consignment credit is the ultimate thrifty-chic maneuver 'cause you are not spending a dime to build the wardrobe of your dreams. Woo-hoo!

Your Contemplate pile will be for those garments you just can't part with yet. The emotional attachment is too strong, and you think you still might be able to use the garment somehow or in some way, though, no doubt, you haven't for quite some time! You may find, at the end of your wardrobe weed, that your Contemplate pile is pretty high. If so, don't be discouraged—it's fine. Again, this is tough stuff.

What I suggest you do is put all of your Contemplate garments at one end of your closet, preferably the far-out-of-reach end, or better yet, in another closet altogether. Give yourself six months. If you do not use your Contemplate garments in that time period, then go ahead and Donate or Re-Create.

A CREATIVE way to hold on to fond memories from old garments is to cut key pieces or fabric swatches from them and make something useful, like a quilt, a pillow, or even a robe. A funny "when I was a party girl" blankie or a "my corporate life" house robe is a hilarious and functional way to pay homage without sacrificing precious closet space.

Your Fits Me Great pile is for just that. Only those garments that flatter your figure, help build shape, and make you feel incredible are to be added to this special heap. This pile will be your *actual* wardrobe. I warn you, this could be a small heap. But keep your fashionable chin up; you are learning so much about yourself as well as developing thrifty-chic skills, confidence, and righteous style muscles that will help you build an incredible Cents of Style wardrobe.

Now that you have cleared space for your piles, know your fit principles, and understand how you are going to separate your garments, it's time to dive in. You should plan to try on as many things as possible and maybe even have a trusted friend lend a hand and an opinion or two. You need to take a strong look at each and every garment in your wardrobe and ask:

- **How is the fit?** Does this follow the guidelines for my body type?

- **Is it flattering?** Be honest! Does this garment work to enhance your figure? Does it look feminine?

• **When was the last time you wore it?** If you haven't worn it in the past year, there is probably a reason why, and I bet it's not 'cause it fits you great.

• **Do you feel great when you wear it?** This is a huge question. I can't stress this enough: when you put on something fabulous, it changes you. I know you know what I am talking about. You feel beautiful, powerful, stylish, and modern. I want you to have a closet full of clothes that you love and that *work* for you and your figure. If you feel great in every single clothing item you own, you will become a more impactful and happy person, guaranteed.

• **Could you wear it in another way or with something else?** Just because it is a part of an "outfit" doesn't mean it has only one use.

• **Can an alteration salvage the garment?** Could you shorten the hem, add darts, create a new neckline, etc.?

• **Does this garment project the image I want to send to the world?** This is a toughie. What does this garment say about you, and do you want to be sayin' that?

In general, you want to hold on to these anchor pieces:

- *Great* fitted suits
- Fitted blazers
- Trousers with straight legs
- A-line or pencil skirts hemmed to the knee
- Basic black dress
- Fitted denim jacket
- Dark boot-cut or straight-leg jeans
- Accessories, accessories, accessories (well-kept scarves, costume jewelry, handbags, belts, and shoes)

It will only take a few garments before you start to see strong patterns in your clothing choices, and I'm not talkin' plaid or floral. Once you can identify your chronic fit and fashion mistakes, you can start to make better choices and become a much better shopper. Understanding why a garment does or doesn't work for you and your body is half the battle, but seeing the issue played out in garment after garment has a way of driving the lesson home.

It often happens that we have a favorite outfit. We don't know why it's our favorite, but we like the way it makes our body look and the way it makes us *feel*. We get a load of compliments on this outfit, and we wear it into the ground. We then proceed to spend years and countless dollars trying to reproduce that outfit, those feelings, and those compliments. But we can never quite create the original magic of that favorite outfit, because we don't really understand why that outfit was so stellar.

Well, once you identify all of the whys, if you will, strategically shopping for stylish bargains that optimize your figure and make you feel incredible becomes a breeze, so you don't have to spend more countless hours or wasted dollars. But you've gotta go through your closet to really understand the whys. You can do this—I know you can! Good luck, and I hope you are knee deep in Fits Me Great.

DENIM CHIC

I want to discuss jeans in the "Closet Evaluation and Organization" chapter because I really want to open your eyes to contemporary denim. Jeans are not the "dungarees" of old;

jeans have become major style statements and a modernizing tool for every wardrobe. There is just one slight *problema* many of us have: bad, bad, bad—I mean *bad*—jeans in our wardrobe.

Jeans! Some would say that jeans are second only to swimsuits as the most frustrating garment to shop for, buy, and wear. I say, nah. You can go years strategically dodging the need for a swimsuit (Alaska is beautiful in the summer, which gives you a twelve-month reprieve from exposing Cool Whip thighs—yippee!), but jeans are a wardrobe necessity. They are the American uniform, and you've simply gotta have 'em. But there are hundreds of different designs, styles, and cuts, and many of us have a closet full of, shall we say, fit misses. Therefore, jeans are the number one shopping challenge in my book.

Jeans serve many wardrobe purposes these days, and some jeans even do tricks. We all have a pair of jeans that are like a security "binky." They are comfortable, they nurture our curves like a pair of PJs, and we can face emotional tasks only with them backing us up. And in every closet, there is a pair of jeans that serve as the ultimate yardstick of weight loss. We gauge every pound by how far our plump thigh can squeeze down the leg and relish the fact that we can get 'em on, up, and zipped.

We all have the same general wish list for our jeans. We want them to make us look taller and leaner, improve our booty, flatten our tummy, and not bruise our bankbook. This can be a tall order for the jeans fairy, as proven by the pile of underused jeans in most women's closets. Great jeans that flatter our individual figures are simply hard to find. But with a few simple tips, wading through our closet's sea of denim can be much easier.

First, let's talk about what general jeans features look best on every body type—and what you have in your closet. If your jeans don't have these features, they are probably not making you feel bootylicious, and I bet they are not your faves either. Jeans are anchor pieces; they're a part of your wardrobe workforce that have the job of building you a fantabulous shape. So your jeans need to *work*. (Insert two snaps, a smirk, and head bobble here.)

Features for Fitting Jeans

Take all of your jeans down, and before you try them on, check each pair for these features:

- **A smile in the front and a frown in the back:** When you lay your jeans out flat, you should notice that the waistband dips down in the front and curves up in the back. This smile in the front is a skinny strategy that visually cuts your tummy in half, deflating your pooch and allowing your shirts and other tops to sit closer to your natural waist.

The frown in the back ensures a more flattering, curve-loving fit by capturing all of your booty for a more comfortable "no plumber butt" fit.

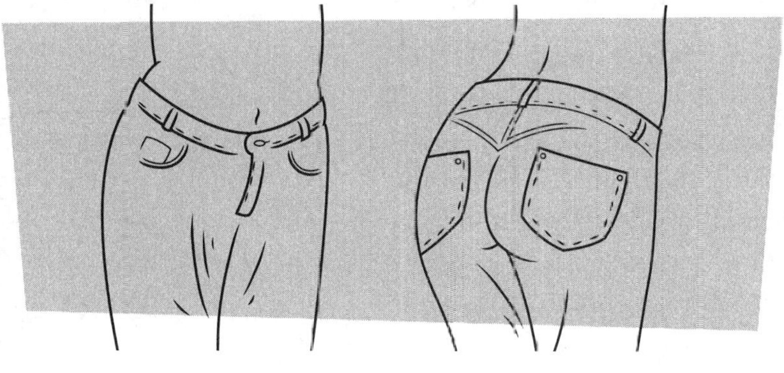

• **Slanted front pockets that reach up like the side of a pyramid:** Slanted pockets help promote the impression of an hourglass shape. Straight pockets that run parallel with the waistband or side seams can make tummies look boxy. (No, thanks!)

• **A zipper about the length of your hand:** Zippers that are the length of your hand from the base of your palm to the tip of your longest finger are generally an indication of a midrise. You'll recall from Chapter 3 that mid-rise trousers, hitting you around the belly button, have the most flattering cut for everyone. Zippers much shorter than your hand are low rise, and much longer than your hand are high rise.

The biggest complaint most women have about modern jeans is the rise. (The rise is the front span of fabric that determines whether your tummy is captured for good keeping, strategically divided for optimal camouflage, or released for spillage.) Most women say they hate low-rise jeans because they expose their tummies—muffin top. Low-rise jeans are also blamed for creating "plumber butt" when you bend over (exposing your coin slot, as the kids say). But high-rise or high-waisted jeans only accentuate a fuller tummy and flatten your booty. A mid-rise jean that divides the tummy in half is simply the most flattering.

• **A larger, defined yoke:** The yoke is the V-shaped panel of fabric below the back waistband. A larger yoke gives the illusion of a smaller booty. This panel creates a curvy fit, allowing the back of your

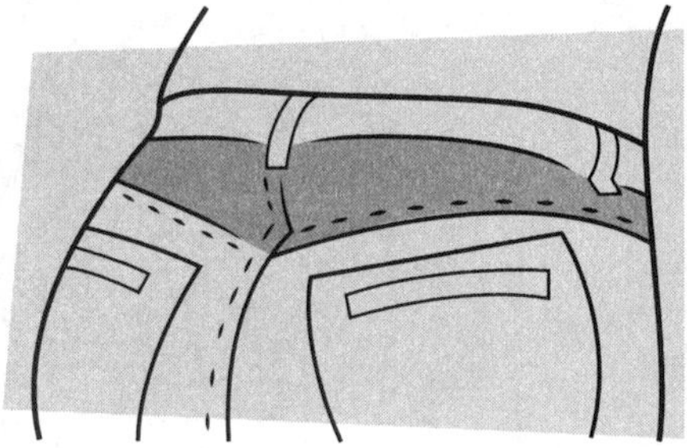

jeans to sit closer to your body. It also divides your bottom into nicely shaped compartments, making it look smaller than it really is. (Yeah for yokes!)

A bigger or deeper yoke means that your trunk will visually have less junk, and the waist will probably fit better.

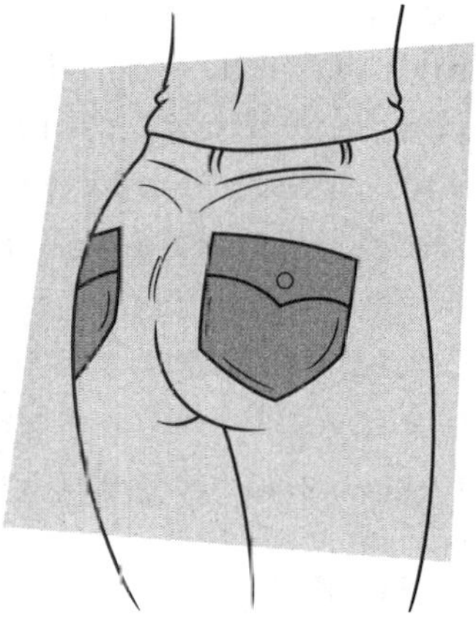

- **Large, slanted back pockets that hit the center of your buns like bull's-eyes:** The larger the pockets, the smaller the butt; the smaller the pockets, the biggah the butt. Avoid pockets that are placed far out on the arse and ones that are too close together. It's also better if they are tilted out just a bit, to give the illusion of plump perfection.

- **Sculpted or triangular pockets:** Square pockets give you a square butt, so stay away from anything square. You want sculpted pockets that are triangular, meaning larger at the top than at the bottom. (This is another better-booty trick.)

- **Straight legs or, better yet, a boot cut:** Tapered, skinny legs make your butt look bigger; if your butt can handle the maximization, go for it. A boot cut is one that tapers in ever so slightly at the knee and then releases to a hem that is just a little wider than the thigh. This is by far the most flattering cut, making your legs look longer and visually balancing the body. But a straight leg can possibly cut the mustard if the circumference of the hem is the same as or close to the circumference of the thigh. Bring the hem to the *seat*, and check it out.

When you have gone through all of your jeans, the ones that do not pass the denim docket will need to be placed in the Donate pile. Stop right now! Do not even think about holding on to those hideous light-colored, overtreated, high-waisted, tapered, and possibly pleated jeans. Even if you were just planning to paint in them while donating your time to Habitat for Humanity, these jeans are fashion atrocities, and the only charitable salvation is Donation.

Those that seem to have all of the right elements will still need to be tried on to make sure that they are true Fits Me Great goods. Put 'em on, give 'em a gander in a full-length mirror, and look for these qualities:

Front

- The waist hits around your belly button without being too tight or causing your tummy to muffin over the top.
- Front pockets lie flat and are nicely angled in and up like an hourglass.
- The crotch ends close to the body without excessive gaping, pulling, or gathering. Check to make sure there is no crotch tent when you sit down.
- The legs offer an elongating line that balances your hips and is not too tight across the thigh. The hem extends at least to the base of the back of your foot.
- Any treatment is subtle. Keep in mind, heavily faded or lighter areas draw the eye and make those areas look larger.

Back

- The yoke is deep and hugs the body. Bend over and check for an underwear salute or, worse, a coin slot how-do-ya-do!
- Beefy back pockets are bun-centered, tilted slightly, and triangular.
- You see two distinctive cheeks that are separated and cradled by perfectly constructed denim.

If your jeans are too big in the waist or are a little too long, you can easily have them altered—Re-Create! But beware, if the jeans in question are more than six inches too long, the fabric allowance for the knee and crotch are probably designed for a taller person, and a simple hem will not fix the fit.

Thrifty Jeans Tips

Of course these fit principles apply to shopping for new jeans as well. Now that you know what to look for, finding a budget pair that fit like a glove is much easier. I have always had incredible luck with finding jeans for all sizes at Old Navy, Sears, JCPenney, H&M, and Wal-Mart. I absolutely love the just-below-the-waist stretch boot cut jeans from Old Navy. Sears and JCPenney always have great deals on Levi's 550 and Lee Natural Fit jeans, and I really like the Metro7 jeans from Wal-Mart. Each of these options offers great fit, prices under thirty bucks, and stylish high-end designs that will totally fool the eye.

But the first step before heading out on your jeans hunt is to consult your retail calendar (as laid out in Chapter 7).

August, September, and January are the best months to find great jeans at bargain prices, because these are "back to school" months, the two times a year when parents make bulk purchases for toddlers, tweens, or teens headed back to campus.

With the average student having eight pairs of jeans in his or her closet, retailers know that there are lots of denim dollars to be spent during these months, and they do a bargain-denim dance to get you into their stores. You are sure to find the widest variety of sizes, styles, and bargain prices during these months, so plan ahead if you can. But if your need for denim has hit at another time of year, don't fret; just apply all of the economic-shopping strategies laid out in Chapter 6. There are still lots of ways to get your favorite jeans for less.

YOU WILL see that I use the terms *denim* and *jeans* interchangeably, but the truth is there is a sort of fashionista chichi-froufrou difference. Just so ya know, jeans are those things that we garden in and do laundry in, the super-casual kind. Denim is that hot, modernizing wardrobe essential that gives us a casual ease. Denim says we didn't try too hard, and we look this great. Jeans say we didn't even try. Get it?

From an economical standpoint, I always advise shopping for the darkest denim you can find. Jeans that are treated to look like they have been dragged behind a truck for a week will always look even worse even faster. Let your own wear and wash create that worn-in look. It will save you money in the long run. Besides, darker denim with little treatment always looks more polished and sophisticated. You want this type of denim for date nights, dress-down Fridays at the office, PTA meetings, and upscale casual functions.

Shopping for jeans that mimic what the high-end designers are doing is one way to build implied value. If two-hundred-dollar jeans have subtle denim treatments, a specific pocket detail and/or shape, or maybe even unique stitching, then finding that same subtlety in a twenty-five-dollar pair will help create the modest-moola magic. This will, of course, make them look richer. But be careful not to buy imitations; simply select jeans that have been inspired by a specific designer or brand.

OPTIMIZING WHAT YOU HAVE

The quickest way to optimize your wardrobe is to organize your closet. Being able to see all of your Fits Me Greats when you open your closet door is a crucial component to thinking more creatively and utilizing garments in a new and different way. Observing all of your fashion potential every time you go into your closet is inspiring and makes you want to be a better dresser, so you need to arrange your closet so that you are visually aware of everything you have.

Your Plastic-Free Closet

There are two ways to save money on your wardrobe: you can spend less or wear your garments longer. Ridding your closet of nonbreathable plastic goes a long way toward preserving the longevity of your wardrobe and getting more bang for your buck. So one of the first things you want to do when taming your closet is to remove all of the plastic that is covering your garments.

Plastic dry cleaners' bags, plastic sweater keepers, and even plastic shoe boxes not only hide what's inside, they also trap dry-cleaning chemicals, perspiration, and general funk in your clothes and shoes. These elements, when trapped, start to break down the fibers of your garments and cause them to pill and look worn much faster.

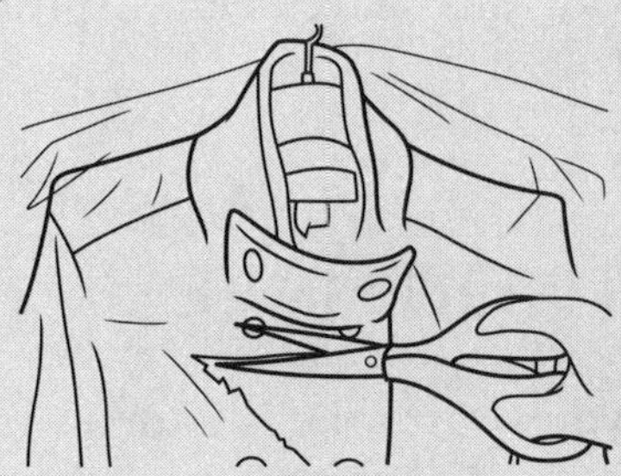

IF YOU live in an old building, as I do, and need the dust protection of a dry cleaner's bag, simply cut the bag shorter, leaving approximately ten inches to cover the top of your garment. Slip it back on your garment, and this trick will protect the shoulders from dust while allowing the garment to breathe when it's hanging in your closet.

Visual Organization

Now that the plastic is gone, separate your garments, and hang all of your pants together, all of your skirts together, your jackets together, and your dresses, tops, shirts, and blouses together. Break up two- and three-piece outfits that usually hang together, including your suits. Additionally, I want you to hang your denim with your trousers. Denim is a modern wardrobe element that should be considered as pants.

Depending on the size and space in your closet, you really want to hang as many things as you can. Items tucked away in drawers are easily forgotten when coordinating a shmaashing outfit, so empty your drawers of any wardrobe essentials, and put them on hangers. Once you have completed this step, go into each section, and organize it by season and color. Hang all of your wool trousers together, all of your linen shirts, cotton skirts, and so on. Lastly, colorblock these subsections. This will make you keenly aware of your wardrobe deficiencies and overages.

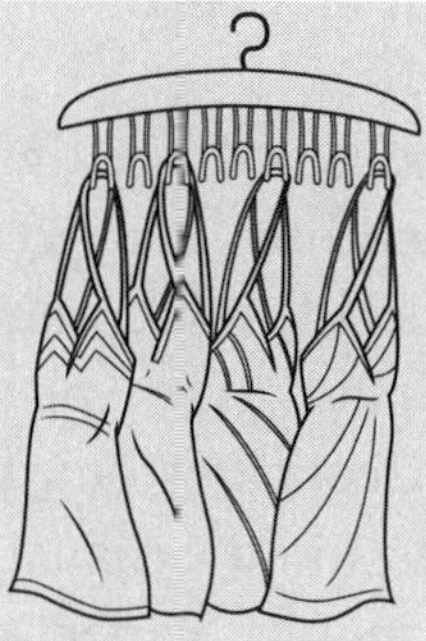

HOOKED BELT hangers make great camisole organizers. Just assign each cami a hook, and you'll be able to see every cam-cam you own and take up a minimal amount of space in your closet.

Just like an artist, you want to blend, layer, and create with as many options as possible when using the garments of your wardrobe. Separating and reorganizing all of these pieces will help you see using them in a fresh new way, ensuring that you are getting your money's worth from your garments and staying far away from a fashion rut.

THOUGH I encourage you to separate and utilize your suits as individual garments, you should never dry-clean or launder them separately. If something were to happen during the chemical process that causes fading, you want it to happen to both pieces. So always clean all pieces at the same time.

Your shoes need the same visual organizing. You want to be able to see your choices when considering an outfit's shoe selection. If you're like me, you keep your boxes. I have more than two hundred pairs of shoes. I have been the same shoe size since the fifth grade, so I have gathered quite a collection in the past twenty years, and I still love sporting some of my retro eighties-chic high school shoes—and most of them have their original box.

The way I keep track of all of my shoes is with digital photographs taped to the outside of each box. I love this method because it keeps my shoes protected in breathable boxes, keeps my closet neatly organized, and gives me the visual cue I need when pondering the perfect city stompers. I do not use expensive photo paper or go to an exhaustive effort; I just take a shot, print it out on regular paper, and tape it to the end of the box. If you are not a box saver, then you want to display your shoe inventory on shoe trees on the back of your closet door, on shoe shelves, or arranged in the bottom of your closet, so you can see your shoes and get to them with ease.

When it comes to your sweaters, it's best to keep them folded and stacked in natural-cotton sweater keepers or on a shelf of your closet. Shelf dividers are a must for piled-high knits on your closet's top shelf. You might not think that shelf dividers are necessary, but if you fear pulling down a mound of knits to get to a sweater at the bottom of the heap, I've got my money on the likelihood you'll just skip it and stick with the cozy fuzzy on top. The shelf dividers help keep everything separated so that you can easily utilize *all* of your stacked sweaters without fear of a knit storm when you reach up and pull one down.

Think about how you can display all of your accessories, handbags, and belts. I have a client who applied cork board to an entire unused wall of her closet and hung all of her necklaces, earrings, and bracelets from stick pins, so she could see all of her fabulous jewelry at a glance—genius! As a result, she wears her beautiful accessories all the time and dresses with much more creativity and less routine. However you choose to store and/or display your accessories, know that the more you see them and have easy access to them, the more they will be utilized in a clever, uniquely fashionable way.

The same goes for all of your wardrobe, for that matter. You need to see what you have to really get your fashion mojo workin'. Plus, all of this organization and easy access will make getting dressed less of a chore and more of a pleasure. As you start to stretch and build your style muscles and dress with more flair, people will notice. You will receive more compliments, which in turn will see you develop more confidence, and you will be further encouraged to make stronger fashion statements. But it all starts with a little organization. You can do it!

6

Bang for the Buck

Shopping and Wardrobe-Building Strategies to Optimize Every Cent

Well, now you know how to fit your fine feminine frame, and arranging a creative toolshed of clothing is just a Saturday away. You've got your undies in order, and you are well versed on what *not* to wear. Now let's talk about how you can build a high-functioning wardrobe that offers a big ol' bang for the buck.

ANCHOR PIECES

The goal of every high-functioning thrifty diva is to gather a wardrobe workforce of anchor pieces, trousers, skirts, and jackets that will serve as the building blocks of your wardrobe, establishing polish, sophistication, and modern femininity. Your anchor pieces are your structural soldiers of shape. These pieces should be solid earth-toned figure makers that balance your body, have little or no adornment, and are made of fabrics that you can wear all year long. Adornment and tchotchke details date your anchor pieces and limit how you can wear them and what you can wear them with.

Anchor pieces would include basic trousers in black, chocolate, gray, khaki, army green, or white, as well as knee-length skirts in the same hues and fitted jackets that sculpt an hourglass the second you slide them on. Dark, sophisticated denim *(wink!)* would also be included in the cast of anchor pieces, and so would the perfect little black dress. All of these garments, when done right, serve as the comfy, dependable style staples that will see you ready for the opera, the movies, the grocery shopping, or the meeting that could change your life. Once you have this flattering collection established, then all you need to stay current and flexible with your look is modern tops and accessories.

A GREAT-FITTING jacket or blazer has magical powers! Throw it on with basic jeans, a top, and a modern pair of shoes, and suddenly you are casual, pulled-together chic. No need to lose that familiar fabulosity during the summer months; just pick up a short-sleeved jacket in a lighter fabric, or better yet, take an underused fitted jacket from your closet, and have the sleeves shortened. To get the perfect length and shape of the sleeves, take in a favorite short-sleeved blouse for the seamstress to copy. You'll get that old-jack(et)-magic feeling again!

Your tops and your accessories will set the mood of your outfit and tell your creative tale. This is both the most economical and the most efficient way to dress your body and maintain a current edge. If the hottest color this season is red, you do not have to run out and snag the latest red suit. Though it would no doubt be gorgeous, you can sell the same visual sophistication by pairing a red top with a rich brown, black, or gray suit, fabulous red shoes, rich printed scarf, structured red handbag, and other coordinated accessories. This is a far more stylish and expressive way to dress, and it is much more cost-effective.

A few seasonless fabrics to consider when shopping for your anchor pieces are tropical wool, gabardine, silk, cotton, denim, polyester blends *(screeching halt!)*—yes, polyester. Fabric technology and the advancements in poly have been so successful that now you really *want* to shop for garments that incorporate a little poly! The truth is, polyester, today more commonly called microfiber, is now a breathable, wicking fabric that is used to make the uniforms of our soldiers, postal carriers, and U.S. Olympians! A little polyester will help a garment keep its shape and color, as

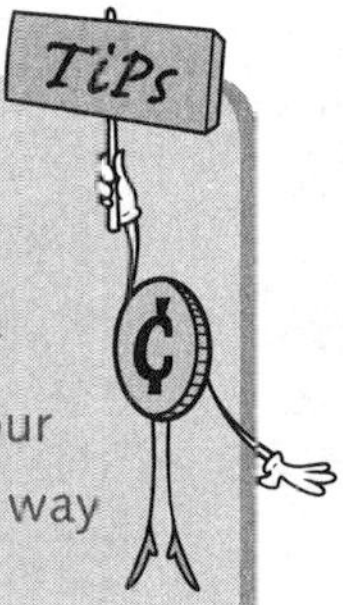

FOR THE most part, accessories do not come in a size, and they do not care how much you weigh (yippee!), so you can utilize fabulous well-cared-for accessories for years to come, no matter how big your booty gets. Thrifty-chic accessories are never a bad way to spend a dollar . . . or two.

well as add to the life of the garment. We are not talking about the stinky, sweaty poly of old. I'm talking about the new poly that can render a "poly-silken" blouse completely undetected in a sea of three-hundred-dollar 100 percent silk blouses. You can hardly tell the difference, so don't be scared of the P word.

THREE THINGS YOU ALREADY OWN

You want to consider your anchor pieces as five-year purchases and your tops and less-structured second layers as one- to two-year purchases. But whether you are looking for basic black britches or a fabulously unique top, you never want to buy anything that you can't visualize wearing with at least three things you already own. This little test will help keep your creative fashion juices flowing, keep your closet free from one-hit wonders, and ensure you maximize your wardrobe scratch.

A great way to think about the three-things-you-already-own rule is to contemplate how you could wear a potential item on Friday night, Saturday afternoon, and Monday morning—basically, Friday night out on a date with your honey, Saturday afternoon out shopping with the girls, and Monday morning to the office. Say you are thinking about buying a great fitted, men's-inspired, pinstriped suit vest. It is a little sexy, is on major sale, and falls within your fashion budget. Before you buy it, think about the things that you have hanging in your closet, and start your creative engine.

How could you wear a tailored yet sexy men's-inspired vest on Friday night out on a date? Maybe atop a ribbed tank or cami with long, dark jeans, high-heeled colored pumps, eye-catching dangly earrings, and a clutch handbag—sexy and a little tough!

How about on a Saturday afternoon with the girls? Pair it with a full skirt cut to the knee, stylish flats, an ethnic scarf looped around your neck, and a great newsboy hat—Bohemian and unexpected!

Now for Monday morning to an office meeting. Think structured black Hepburn trousers, crisp white shirt, graphic scarf knotted like a man's tie against your neck, and fabulous brick-red accessories—powerful yet classic and feminine.

Now, not only are you ready to commit to the vest, you are ignited to wear it in all the ways you envisioned. That thrifty-chic vest has the potential to make a fashionable impact on your wardrobe and your social calendar. But the key to these stylish visions is the fact that well-fitting anchor pieces—like long, dark denim, A-line skirts cut to the knee, and elegant trousers—are hanging in your closet, waiting to help you paint your fashion picture. This is how you make dressing fun, enjoyable, and creative.

When you have the comfortable confidence of knowing that your anchor pieces are working for you—that they are creating a great shape and offering implied value—you can then relax and enjoy the process of decorating your body and expressing your creative spirit through your tops and accessories. Honoring your inner fashionista becomes second nature!

THE SPORT OF SHOPPING

The way I see it, shopping is a sport! The more you train, study, and strategize, the better prepared you'll be to spot, pounce on, and bag the bodacious bargains! Understanding your body, what looks best on it, what your wardrobe is missing, and what key items could help you optimize what you already have are all shopping bees that should be buzzing around your bargain bonnet.

Keeping a running list of items that you actually need and things that will help you get more wear out of garments you already own is essential. A simple folded index card of jotted-down items, kept in your wallet—*in front* of your credit card—will keep you focused when you enter a store and remind you of what your wardrobe priorities are before you "swipe" your budget away.

The ultimate key to a bargain is *time*: time to find the right stores to shop in, time to wait for some things to go on sale, time for the hunt, and a little time to think about whatcha really need before you plop down the plastic. Rarely is an impulse buy a good one. We all get frustrated with not finding what we really want, not liking what we see, and just needing to get the heck out of the store before we have a spastic fit of fashion failure and pledge to go naked for the rest of our lives. But if you spend a little more time and have a plan, you can spend a lot less money.

Before you buy another garment to put into your beautifully organized closet, make sure you have the essentials. Again, an effective wardrobe of great-fitting, earth-toned anchor pieces will see you through any occasion. If you are missing these items, add them to your list and start there. Apply these shopping principles when building your Cents of Style wardrobe:

Wardrobe-Building Strategy Checklist

- Never buy anything that you can't visualize wearing with at least three things you already own.
- Never buy anything that you don't absolutely love—I mean it; just don't do it!
- Never buy anything that doesn't fit right and feel comfortable.
- Shop for fabrics that you can wear year-round.
- Choose classic-cut garments with little adornment for your anchor pieces (pants, skirts, and jackets).
- Choose colorful, expressive tops that send a fashionable message, enhance skin tone, and complement your eyes.

This little list will help eliminate those "I have nothing to wear this with" items that never see the outside of your closet!

Dodging those needless purchases and gathering your wardrobe workforce is empowering. Being fashionably prepared for anything and looking shmaashing doing it offer a peace of mind that an impulse buy just can't offer. Simply put, a winning wardrobe workforce wallops a wad of one-hit wonders every time!

SALE RACK

So let's talk about the sale rack, that beautiful rainbow of discounted fashion magic or that mangled mess of last season's crap. However you look at it, the sale rack is the fashion flint that ignites a true thrifty diva. Now, there are lots of reasons why garments end up on the sale rack, and a keen understanding of these variables helps a good bargain shopper elevate her game to the realm of the powerful shopper hero.

Wallflowering: Your Best Money-Saving Strategy

Now, when you enter a store, there is a distinct and cost-effective way to approach "the goods." Most of us head in and are immediately taken with all of the shiny new high-priced happy threads perfectly displayed to tempt your fashion fancy. Sure enough, you'll find that the most expensive and perfectly organized duds hang in the front of the store, preening like peacocks and tugging at your wallet. But if you can possibly go in with blinders, head to the back of the store, and work your way forward, you'll find much better deals.

I call this strategy "wallflowering," as you are sure to find more blooming bargains, the closer you get to the walls. Keep your eyes peeled for the sale signs, and keep moving till you reach the sale racks. The simple habit of shopping the back of a store forward and heading to the sale rack first can save you an average 25 percent on your total wardrobe budget over a year. It seems so simple, but wallflowering blooms beaucoup bucks of savings, so keep on truckin' till you hit the racks in back!

Prepare for a Mess

When it comes to sale racks, you need to understand that most of them look like a bomb hit 'em. They are an ignored, unorganized mess that represents less profit for retailers, so sales associates do little to keep them tidy and orderly. But a thorough sweep of the marked-down glad rags is a must. This becomes effortless once you know what looks best on you and what you really need. As you are sifting through, remember a bigger mess means you're sure to spend less!

Month-Old Items

In many discount stores, items hit the sale rack simply because they've been in the store for a couple of weeks, and new merchandise takes precedence. For the most part, retailers want items to be cleared out every few weeks. So if a garment is in a store for more than thirty days, quite often it hits the bargain bin for *no other* reason than time.

Something else to consider, and another justification for shopping the sale rack first, is that designers do not reinvent the wheel every season. If designers find that they've created a great skirt or trousers that fit well and generate good feedback from buyers, they will use the same pattern in a different fabric for the next few seasons. So on occasion, you can find *very* similar garments from a designer hanging on the sale rack in the back and being sprightly sported on a pristine rack in the front of the store.

Returned or Damaged Items

Returned items and slightly damaged items usually end up on the sale rack as well. These items also reflect a time schedule for turnover, and retailers want to see them gone. If something looks worn or damaged, you can negotiate for a deeper discount. Just ask!

Mis-Sizing

Now, I am going to let you in on a huge industry secret—and this one's a shocker, so get ready! One of the biggest reasons why garments end up on the sale rack and designer duds see their way straight to discount stores is mis-sizing. Mis-sizing is one of those little-known phenomena that allow us to take advantage of great bargains, *if* we are willing to ignore the number hanging in our britches and just focus on the fabulously discounted goods.

The truth is, most of the garments that we wear are not made in this country, and sizing mistakes due to language issues, fabric-cutting issues, and other business errors happen more than you realize. Don't get me wrong: designers go to great lengths to ensure that this doesn't happen, but it does—all the time.

Not only does mis-sizing happen by accident, it often happens due to textile issues. For example, say a designer ordered four thousand yards of fabric to make a specific pair of trousers that is sure to satisfy hundreds of buyers with preorders. During shipment of the fabric, maybe there is a hurricane in the Gulf, and a third of the fabric is ruined due to water damage. The designer now has to stretch the remainder of the fabric to meet all of the orders. So all of the seams in production have to be shaved by a half inch or more to make up for the lost fabric.

Now when you go to try on those fabulously discounted trousers from your favorite designer and the size you normally wear fits too tight, you immediately think it's your Sunday pancakes with extra butter and syrup talkin'. You start beating up your big-butted self! You refuse to go up a size in the britches, even though they are deliciously cheap, because you don't want to think about possible weight gain, and having a larger size hanging in your closet is the worst skeleton you can imagine. Well, you just let your ego "shop-block" a bargain, and your pancakes had *nothing* to do with it.

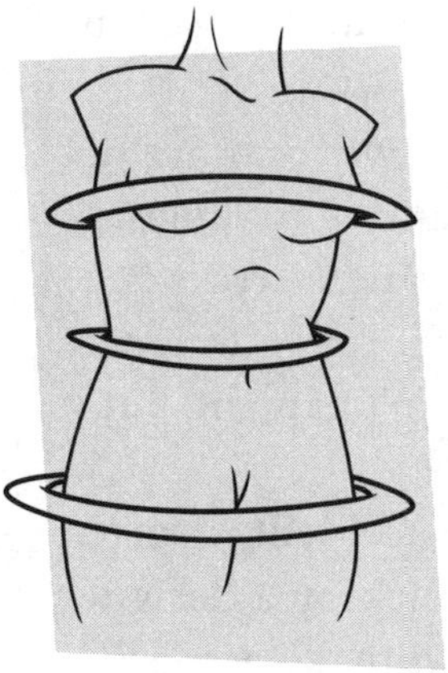

There are so many variables that go into creating a garment that you simply cannot let the number stamped on the label affect your final purchases. Knowing your bust, waist, and seat (low-hip) measurements and having a tape measure handy allow you to quickly measure across a garment to determine if it could work for you, based on *your* numbers and not the designer's. This little trick will also save you valuable time in the dressing room.

In my closet right now, I have clothes that fit me perfectly, ranging from size 6 to size 16. *My* numbers remain the same, but I do not let my ego or the number on the dang tag prevent me from bagging a bargain. Who cares about the number in the garment; it is your numbers that matter—and if you do care, cut the tag out!

Know Your Numbers!

Never go shopping without your trusty tape measure. Whenever you see a garment that you might want to try on, measure the seat or the bust, depending, to see if it will fit comfortably or if you need to go up or down a size.

For example, I know that my seat or low-hip measurement is 40 inches, so a garment must measure at least 20 to 21 inches across the front seat to fit me well and look flattering. Then I measure the length to determine if it will hit me at a flattering place. I know that the best skirt length on me is 25 inches and no more than 27 inches, so if a skirt measures longer, I will need to add alteration costs to the final price. Knowing your measurements and the lengths and widths of your best-fitting garments can save you time in the fitting room.

Sale Rack Tips

- Go to the sale rack immediately when you enter a store.
- Understand that the sale rack in most stores is a disaster! A thorough sweep of *all* garments is a must.
- Recognize that if it is on the sale rack, mis-sizing could be the issue.
- Know your numbers, and bring your tape measure.
- Make sure you look at garments labeled one size larger and one size smaller than you think you are.
- Look for end-of-season bargains that can be worn year-round (for example, denim, tropical wool, gabardine, and lightweight polyester).

FIT: THE REAL SECRET TO BUDGET FASHION MAGIC

There are many variables that ultimately determine a garment's final price, but don't ya just wonder what the real difference is between budget garments and designer garments? I mean, if you have two seemingly identical white, 100 percent cotton, button-up blouses of the same size, how can one be priced at $19.99 and the other at $199.99? What's the real difference? Well, for the most part, it is fabric and fit.

In the beginning of the book, I talked briefly about my years as a fit model. *Fit* is one of those fashion enigmas that few understand and fewer know how to financially circumvent so it just looks like you bought the $199.99 blouse and not the $19.99 one. To really understand this, you need to know a little about the design process, so here goes.

When a designer sits down and sketches designs for an upcoming season, that visual wish list is handed to a pattern maker whose job it is to create a production pattern and a sample version of the design. The pattern maker creates both the pattern and sample garments using body measurements representing the center of the sizing scale for that designer. The center of the sizing scale is usually a size 8 to 12, so garments can easily be graded up and down with fewer production inconsistencies.

These sample garments are first fit on a manikin form. Then a human fit model with the same measurements, knowledge of pattern making, and garment construction is brought in to fit the production samples and ensure that ladies throughout the land can live their life comfortably in those clothes. A fit model brings a garment to life and makes sure it will work and move in the real world.

Well, I was one of those fit models for years, and I was quite successful because my body represented an economical standard that's very appealing to most designers. You see, I'm smaller busted and have a boyish shape without a lot of curves, which means fitting a garment on my body required fewer darts, seams, tucks, and gathers. All of these elements make a garment more expensive to create, so my thicker shape saves a bundle in production.

Now, a budget fashion house will fit a garment on a fit model once and send it into production, gambling somewhat that the general fit will work on most body types and that the adjustments were made correctly on the sample garments. But a designer house will painstakingly fit a garment to visual perfection before things get mass-produced. Often two, three, or more fittings will be employed to ensure that all of the elements meet the designer's specs and all seams and darts fall in the right place to create a consummate garment and beautiful fit. Therefore, the outcome is a more detailed and costly fit.

With this understanding, you, the thrifty diva, can create that designer look by purchasing budget garments and doing the last round of fittings yourself! In other words, if you buy that $19.99 blouse, you can create a $199.99 look by having the blouse tailored to your body. Adding the seams and darts that allow the garment to skim the body, create an hourglass shape, and visually create a polished look will make the garment appear much more high-end. This $10 to $20 investment will elevate the entire look of the garment and sell it as a much more expensive blouse!

Tailoring and altering your garments so they work for your unique body is the real secret to budget fashion magic. When a garment masterfully fits your hot body, making you look longer, leaner, more curvaceous and feminine, framing your assets like the Mona Lisa, you are looking like a million without spending a fortune. So you have a choice: you can pay for the fit model and fashion house to do the extra fittings, or you can go cheap, do the fitting yourself, and get the designer look for lots less!

WHAT ABOUT a sewing class? Sewing skills are endlessly handy, and it doesn't get more frugally fashionable than an original design. *So cool!* Just think of all the money we could save and how unique we could all look if we dames started sewing again! Sewing classes are often offered through local fabric stores, and both new and used sewing machines can be found online for under fifty bucks! Come on, you can do it!

WHEN IS A CHEAP ITEM NOT A BARGAIN? BUDGET VERSUS DESIGNER DUDS

Another thing to think about when it comes to budget frocks versus designer duds is that you can't copyright a fashion design, so knockoffs are never far behind a successful designer look. Believe me when I tell you that this is the absolute bane of many designers' existence, because there are hundreds of budget fashion houses that do nothing but copy designer styles every season.

Sure as Christmas and sugar, at the end of every designer runway, there are dozens of "press" photographers feverishly shooting the painstaking fashion efforts of designers and their crews of hundreds. A large majority of these photogs can't make it back to the cyber cafe fast enough to upload and sell their images to budget fashion houses all over the world. These smokin'-fresh pics will see reproductions created within days and delivery to your local stores within weeks, right behind the delivery of the original designer duds, and there ain't a darn thing that anyone can do about it—it's just a dirty part of the biz.

Though admittedly unfair, knockoff or budget garments are a bonus for the thrifty. A tailored budget garment with designer elements can offer a thousand-watt look on a generator budget, so keeping up with what your favorite designers are doing each season is a must. You will often find me fluttering around high-end boutiques and exclusive department stores, shopping for a little *perspective.* When you have a firm understanding of what's flying off the shelf at Saks, you can more easily translate that info when you're shoppin' the sale rack at Sears.

Of course, when I say budget garment, I do not mean cheap, and there *is* a difference. A poorly constructed garment will always look cheap, no matter how much you pay for it. Puckered seams, prints that don't match up or go all the way around a garment, zippers that don't lie flat, bad button alignment, and uneven hems are all signs of the cheap stuff. Every now and then, you come across a cheap-looking designer garment, but for the most part, the budget goods are the ones to watch.

Understanding a designer look is all about the details; that is exactly what you need to examine before you make a budget purchase. Just because you are paying less for a garment that doesn't have a high-end designer's name on the tag doesn't mean that you have to sacrifice basic workmanship. You want to check the seams, look for crooked sewing, and make sure the zipper (if there is one) lies flat and doesn't pucker. If there is a pattern to the garment, make sure it meets at the seams and continues all the way around the garment. Also, look for overall symmetry in the hems, sleeve length, etc.

When executed well, these construction details build implied value and help you maintain the monetary mystery. You can absolutely find well-made garments at the bargain end of the fashion spectrum; you just need to avoid the cheap ones. So when you're hankerin' for hip haute couture, here's how to get the look you desire from your favorite bargain basement.

Tips for Budget Garments/Knockoffs

- Budget garments are cut more sparingly, so be prepared to go up a size or two.
- Make sure to check the seams before you buy the garment. The seams are where shoddy workmanship shows.
- Go window-shopping in the upscale boutiques to keep up with the latest trends.
- Remove the garment from the rack of a bargain store, and visualize it hanging in a more upscale boutique.
- Don't get caught up in designer hype. A great knockoff is just days away.

THE BEST PLACES TO SHOP AND WHY

When it comes to finding the best places to get major mileage out of your moola, I say why limit yourself to only a few types of stores? You never know what you'll find at any store, so honoring a basic curiosity can often save you in ways you would've never thought of. In every store, no matter the price points, there is a little to be learned.

Ethnic Enclaves

I love exploring hidden gems in ethnic-rich areas like Chinatown in New York, Little Armenia in Los Angeles, or Little Havana in Miami. Areas such as these offer a great opportunity for shoppers to bypass one of the importing and markup steps. These shops are importing directly from their home country and not working through an import house. As a result, you can save 50 to 75 percent on cool accessories and clothing.

Every major city has these celebrated enclaves of culture, and the bargains are phenomenal. But you have to be willing to go in and take a look around. Once you've dropped by, look at things with a discriminating eye. Key items representing a specific culture can add flavor and unique style to an ensemble, but you never want to look like you are wearing a costume. Skip the warrior headdress, and opt for things like vibrant printed scarves, chunky wood bangles, or full, decorative skirts. One thrifty-chic ethnic piece can speak volumes.

Discount Stores

Discount stores such as T.J. Maxx, Marshalls, and Ross are always great, because you can often find your favorite designer duds for pennies on the dollar. But remember that items often end up at these discount stores for many reasons. These stores buy closeouts, overstock, returned items, mis-sized items, and manufacturers' defects. Some of these stores even have their own private "designer" labels that are made exclusively for the discount store.

Using your shopping strategies at a discount store is crucial, as these stores are ruled by the next shipment. Prices are always set by the amount of time an item has been in the store, and you are possibly dealing with garment gremlins you can use to your advantage. Discount stores can offer a bargain bonanza for an educated shopper, but they can also be a minefield of tacky fashion mishaps if you don't apply the principles of good garment construction.

Consignment Shops

Consignment shops are some of my favorite stores in the world. These little emporiums of gently used gems are fabulous resources for your wardrobe workforce. Consignment shops are privately owned, and the good ones are chock-full of clean, in-season garments that are organized like high-end boutiques.

Most consignment shops contract a fifty-fifty or forty-sixty split on garments that they take in on consignment, and all owners know that every consigner is a potential customer and vice versa, so you're sure to get great customer service. I've honed great relationships with consignment shop owners over the years, and many have helped me ride the fashion wake of some opulent style mavens all over New York City.

Once owners know your style and size and can recognize a pattern of whose garments you tend to purchase, many of them will happily give you a call to let you know when great items from that consigner come in. The absolute best consignment scenario is when you are both a consigner and customer and you can do your shopping on store credit. Now, that is a thrifty diva workin' the system. (Woo-hoo!)

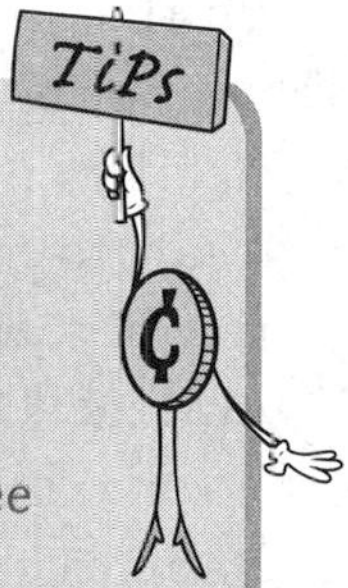

DON'T SHY away from secondhand shoes. A woman's foot grows when she gets pregnant and often never shrinks back, forcing a whole new shoe wardrobe. For this and other fit issues, you can find fabulous once-worn shoes on consignment for a wee bit of wampum.

Thrift Stores

Thrift stores can be a creative field of dreams for the devoted shopper hero. A thrift store will sap your time, but it'll never sap your *dinero*. Thrift stores are usually connected to a charity and take in donated items in any ol' condition. If you are lucky, things are organized by color and garment type, but a boutique it ain't.

As you know, you have to spend a little more time if you plan on spending less money, and a thrift store epitomizes this principle. Every thrifty diva I know has a fabulous thrift store find in her closet with a needle-in-a-haystack tale to tell, but you've got to be up for the hunt. Thrift store items will need to be cleaned, they can't be returned, and many stores do not offer fitting rooms. One easy way around this little caveat is to shop in a thin tee and skirt, so you can slip on tops and easily try on bottoms.

Outlet Malls

Outlet malls have become the Disneyland of bargain-shopping destinations. Many outlets bus people in from nearby cities, offering coupons and free lunch at the food court to get people to come and save some dough, but shopper heroes need to beware of price tag tomfoolery at the outlets. Designer outlets can be awesome, don't get me wrong, but more and more often, you find lower-quality items that were made specifically for the outlet and not premium overstock items, as used to be the case.

Outlets also cleverly price items in multiples to disguise the lack of discount off the regular retail price. For example, you could find a sign advertising two tees for $29.99, when the retail price is $14.99 each. A good outlet offers at least 30 percent off the manufacturer's retail price and has recent-season merchandise.

If you are jonesing for a specific in-season designer item, the outlet is possibly the best way to buy it for less. But no matter where you shop, always use your shopping strategies, and you are sure to spend less and get more of what you need and want.

JUST ASK: QUESTIONS FOR YOUR SALESCLERK OR SHOP OWNER

The people who work in your favorite stores can be an essential component of saving some scratch. Being nice to and getting to know the salesclerks, managers, and shop owners is a friendly way of cracking the shell of inside sale info! These people know when things are coming in and when items are going on sale. They can offer additional discounts and be sweetly persuaded to hold sale items, even when they are not supposed to.

Being nice is certainly important, but it's also significant to realize that the desire to save money is a common denominator for us *all*! No matter how much or how little we have, we all enjoy spending less. It's a fact that we can all agree upon, bond over, and connect with. So taking the initiative to ask for a deeper discount, inquire if something will soon be going on sale, or investigate when there's a secret friends-and-family discount day should not be an embarrassment! A purchase should *never* be made without inquiring whether there are additional discount possibilities.

I can't tell you how many times I've asked the checkout person if there were any coupons or additional discounts that I was unaware of, and within seconds, a little coupon was pulled out of a drawer or the lady behind me offered up a crumpled bar code that, when scanned, produced a surprise discount! Let's face it, we don't always have time to read every ad in the Sunday paper or check the junk mail for special *preferred* customer coupons, but we can simply ask if we've missed something.

Being thrifty is beautiful, and spending less is something to celebrate! If you feel a little uncomfortable or cheap at first, mention how you love shopping at the store because you always seem to find the best deals. We all feel smarter and positive about shopping in a store that offers us great value, and there is nothing cheap about that. Make fun conversation about the twenty-dollar game (read on), or recruit the salespeople to help you find the missing pieces in your wardrobe workforce. The staff of any store is there to help you, and I can assure you, they'd rather help you save money than restock or organize the sweaters. Just ask!

THE TWENTY-DOLLAR GAME

My super-favorite shopping strategy is the twenty-dollar game. I, of course, made up this game, but it is more fun than Old Maid ever dared to be. I liken it to a thrifty-diva scavenger hunt. I actually developed this many years ago

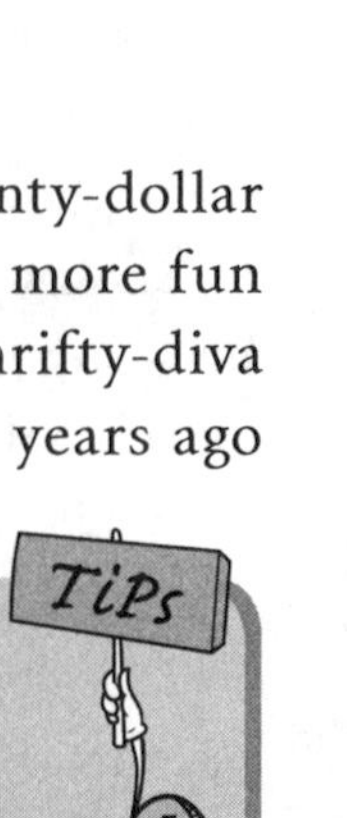

CHECK OUT the junior department for trendy tops and accessories. Juniors live for the latest looks, and you are sure to find less-expensive items in this area.

when I was a struggling college student, and I have never given it up, because it brings me so much joy and inspires such fabulous finds.

The twenty-dollar game is allowing yourself twenty dollars a week in mad money. It's your own tiny stash for a kicky no-guilt purchase. You can buy anything that you want with it, and the bargain hunt for your weekly indulgence is sure to be thrilling. It also helps sharpen your shopper-hero skills. Sometimes you're sure to find something right away, and sometimes you can save up for a couple of weeks if you're really busy.

I've found that the twenty-dollar game is a lot cheaper than Prozac, and knowing that I'm giving myself a gift each week and the freedom to discover what that gift may be is the best shopping therapy there is! I play the twenty-dollar game all of the time, and as a result, I have an entire wardrobe of fabulous twenty-dollar items that I pull together to create thrifty-chic looks for under a hundred dollars every day.

These tips, strategies, and checklists will whip a wardrobe into shape without denting your wallet. All of these strategies take a little time, but remember, it is not about filling your closet with clothes you never wear. It is about making better choices and loving what you have. Rushing and making snap decisions have filled your closet with clothes you hate, so slow down, hummingbird. I'd rather see you have three pairs of awesome britches that make you look incredible than a dozen pairs taking up space in your closet and fooling you into thinking you have more than you really do.

Make your list of wardrobe needs, and give it a glance before you head into the store. Stay focused on the sale rack, the fit, garment construction, fabric, and need. As with any other skill, the more you practice these steps, the faster they will become second nature, and the easier shopping and big-bargain bagging will become. Being a hot chick with a great Cents of Style rocks—enjoy it!

7

Mark Your Calendar

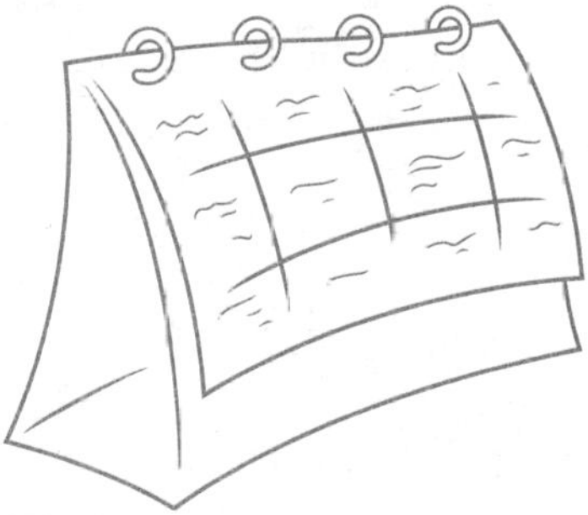

TIMING IS EVERYTHING, and all shopper heroes know that for every bargain, there is a season. Impromptu parties, spontaneous rendezvous in Vegas, and camping excursions on the Appalachian Trail will never find you fashionably amiss if you follow your retail calendar and consciously build a functional wardrobe that'll see you prepared for any situation with style. Knowing when you can save the most on what is an inside retail secret that will have you pinching your pennies with ease and pleasure.

THE WEDNESDAY ADVANTAGE

Attention, all thrifty divas! The ticket to shopping sanity is Wednesday morning; you'll find better parking, fewer shoppers, reorganized racks, more sales help, shorter lines, and bigger bargains. National department stores and big-name chains use Monday and Tuesday to analyze weekend sales and formulate markdowns for midweek. Retailers never want to be stuck with sluggish merch, so price cuts can often be deep midweek to get merchandise moving, rendering it gone by the weekend.

Wednesdays are simply a bargain shopper's delight. As you stroll the organized aisles, unencumbered by people and shopping carts, enjoy the kind customer service of unstressed sales help, and relish the opportunity to snag freshly reduced items, you'll wonder why anyone would darken the door of a store on a Saturday. So make a plan, and enjoy extra-long lunches on hump day. Your wallet and blood pressure will thank you.

JANUARY

Mark your calendar, and start stashing your scratch now. January is the month for winter power shopping. I love January; it's too cold to play outside, and all of the stores are full of red-hot bargains. Yep, end-of-the-year clearances and post-holiday merchandise bloat are everywhere, and if you received a gift card for the holidays, January is the perfect time to use it. (Be sure to check and see if your gift card has an expiration date! Many of them now do.)

January is the time to shop for the following:

- **Boots!** Every style imaginable is on sale, so buy the best pair of leather boots you can afford. You will ultimately get years more wear out of leather boots, because you can have them resoled and polished when they start to look worn. This isn't always the case with faux leather.

- **Outerwear of every variety:** If you have wanted a new coat, parka, or even a suede blazer, you are sure to find amazing deals in January.

- **Winter wraps, scarves, hats, and gloves:** These will perk up your winter cloak for the last wicked days of winter.

- **Anything Christmas red:** Red sweaters, jackets, and pajamas will look great for Valentine's Day. *(Wink!)*

- **Colorful, soft, lightweight sweaters, shrugs, and wraps:** These are not to be overlooked, as they can be worn with sundresses on cool nights during the spring and summer.

- **Anchor garments (trousers, skirts, and jackets):** Well-made garments of tropical wool, gabardine, and lightweight poly blends in basic tones like black, brown, and gray should be on your bargain-shopping brain in January. These go-to garments of your wardrobe workforce offer structure and shape. They are also worn all year long.

- **Denim:** Our daily uniform, offering modern casual ease, always goes on sale when the kids go back to school after the holidays.

- **Camisoles:** Look for unique, feminine, fitted camisoles in lace, satin, or silk. These will work as great day-to-evening pieces for the rest of the year.

- **Sexy sequin tops:** These can be paired with jeans and a fitted blazer for a special night out.

- **Special-occasion dresses:** The sale racks are full of party dresses that didn't see a New Year's Rockin' Eve. If you have an upcoming prom, gala, or wedding to attend this spring, run, don't walk to the special-occasion sale rack of your local department store in January.

IF YOU'RE a bride-to-be, check out the special-occasion sale rack in January for possible deep discounts on dresses that could double as bridesmaid dresses. If there is something you like, the department store can always do a national search for the sizes needed and have them shipped to the ladies. You never know unless you look!

FEBRUARY

You will find cozy clothes and loungewear on the 50 percent–off rack in February, just in time for the coldest part of winter. Fleece-lined, terry cloth, velour, and basic cotton warm-up suits are the last to go on sale at the end of the season, so February is when you stock up. These comfy two-piece throw-ons are considered winter gear, but the truth is, we wear them all year long.

The terry cloth variety serve us well during the summer months, so keep your eyes peeled for those, and always opt for a bright color. You will feel more perky and stylish if you are sporting a fabulous unexpected hue during your downtime.

Be sure to choose straight-leg styles—no tapered pants or, worse, elastic at the ankle—and zip-front hoodies that hit around your hip bone—nothing too long or droopy. Flattering loungewear is a wardrobe necessity, and knowing you look great no matter the occasion or circumstance does a lot to affect your mood. So this is the time to cast off your oversized T-shirts and baggy sweatpants and go for cozy clothes you're excited to put on. You will find them for pennies on the dollar in February.

February is also the month that most lingerie manufacturers and department stores hold "bra events." Valentine's Day lends itself to giving a stronger look at your lingerie drawer, so many stores oblige the need for new undies with buy-one-get-one events. If your favorite bra is an expensive one, mark your calendar, 'cause if they are going on sale at all, it will be in February.

As February and winter wind down, the clearance rack in every store will become more, shall we say, dramatic. By this time, we are ready for new spring things, and we have a tendency to want to rush the season with purchases that evoke a warmer climate, but hit those sale racks first. The 75 percent–off signs will be proudly displayed, and sale merchandise will look disheveled and unorganized, as if it's screaming for help. Stay focused, and remember that the bigger the mess, the bigger the bargains. Holiday returns continue to trickle in through February, so no matter how ruffled the racks, give them a once over.

Fall/winter fashion always generates timeless, classic looks that are slow to go on sale. Many of these will translate into spring and work all year long. Look for these classic items on the February sale rack:

- **Tuxedo vests and menswear-inspired items:** Every season, a few hot designers sprinkle their collection with sexy menswear pieces, so these have become wardrobe classics. (Remember how to rock that vest; see Chapter 6.)

- **Shirts:** Look for crisp, tailored button-up shirts that can be worn with trousers or pencil skirts to work.

- **Winter white:** Choose items like lightweight wool pants that will look fresh for spring.

- **Feminine, flow-y tops:** These can be toughened up with boot-cut jeans or summer cargos.

- **Accessories, accessories, accessories!** Clutch handbags, chandelier earrings, silky scarves, large statement pendants, and belts are all being cleared out in February for new, fresh things. Grab 'em while you can at a major discount; they will add to your accessory wardrobe, and you can use them all year long.

- **Boots:** If you didn't buy boots in January, don't miss the opportunity in February! Every shoe store imaginable will offer give-'em-away discounts on boots. Look for all kinds of boots: snow boots, rain boots, knee-high, ankle. All of them denote a wintertime shoe, and with spring only a couple of weeks away, retailers will be clearing them out.

MARCH

In March, the stores they start a-wooing! The sprout of spring makes all of us itch for something new, bright, and fun, but real bargain shoppers know that the stores are currently stocked to the rafters with full-price (eek!) items that should be dodged like doughnuts before a class reunion.

Retailers realize that many of us are waiting for a better bang for our buck, so they've started enticing us with spring preview coupons that offer a decent savings. Keep your eyes peeled for the discount dividends to hit your mailboxes and e-mail in-boxes in March.

March is a good month to shop the sale rack for trousers and pants. The stores are currently stocked with full-price skirts and dresses, because women tend to wear more of those in the spring and summer, so the pants get pushed to the sale rack. When you hit the sale rack looking for bargain britches, remember these guidelines:

- To optimize your money, shop for fabrics that you can wear all year long (tropical wool, poly blends, heavier cotton blends, gabardines, etc.).

- Skip the pleats. Pleats were created so that men would have a place to put their golf balls while on the course. Most women do not need the extra fabric and ballooning around the middle that pleats create.

- Say no to tapered legs. Straight-leg pants that cleanly fall from the largest part of your bottom are always a much more flattering option.

- Pass up the high waist. High-waist pants bring attention to your tummy. The best fit is a waist that falls just around the belly button.

Because March offers a fashion smorgasbord of bright, fresh colors, textures, styles, and patterns that are magically alluring this time of year, I encourage you to shop for perspective! Gather the knowledge of all things new, and then apply what you learn to what you already have. Take stock of your closet, and establish what still fits, what you can mix and match to create new looks, and what key items you'll need to pull things together with a modern edge. Great tops and the latest accessories can update everything. Remember, fabulous clothing bargains are just a couple of weeks away!

A FEW elite designers create a small cruisewear line for warmer climates during the winter. These lines offer a sneak peek at what summer has to offer, and if there are any garments left, they hit the sale rack in March.

Though March isn't the thriftiest fashion month on the calendar, this span of fashion purgatory does offer a few unexpected bargains in other arenas. With spring break in full gear and summer vacations just around the corner, March is the time to find great deals on luggage and all things travel. Look for competitive bargains on sleeping bags, folding chairs in a bag, camping supplies, and duffle bags. Large discount stores have been flooded with these items, and bargain wars are sure to be found!

APRIL

April is one of the best months to shop your local consignment and resale boutiques. Many women are cleaning out their closets in April (maybe you should, too!) to make room for new things, and these stores are brimming with recycled riches just waiting to be discovered. Barely worn items that just didn't work out for one person could be exactly what you are looking for. So plan to stop by your local thrift or resale store in April; you may be pleasantly surprised.

Once the spring holidays pass, spring sales start to bloom. Here's what to look for during the latter half of April:

- **Dresses:** Many stores pack the racks, preparing for the yearly craving of a new Easter or Passover dress. Hop quickly like a bunny at the end of April to find great dresses reduced and on the sale rack.

- **Raincoats:** If you've been hankering for a fabulous bright-colored raincoat, the end of April is the time to buy it. The stores want them out of sight before May.

- **Knit, knit, knit:** In just a few weeks, many knits are going to feel too heavy in summer's heat, so stores push them out in April.

- **Luggage:** The stores overstock luggage for spring breakers, so look for delightful discounts that will get these bulky items moving. Luggage eats valuable retail space, and once spring break is "broke," stores want them gone.

MAY

In May we celebrate with dutiful bliss all the wonders of our mothers, and the leftover retail items that didn't get wrapped up for her hit the sale rack with lightning speed on the Monday after her big day. This retail week, you'll find beaucoup bargains on the items that weren't given to Mom.

May is also the month for closeout linens and bedding. New styles will be introduced for fall and back to school, so stock of last year's designs is priced to fly. Head to the sale rack first, and look for great buys on these items:

- Sleepwear: cozy robes, slippers, pajamas, and nightgowns
- Bath and body sets: collections of pampering spa goodies that ease the body and spirit
- Gold and diamond jewelry
- Perfume gift sets
- Blooming flowers: all of the special potted plants that were grown to bloom in May
- All things with a mother theme: picture frames, jewelry, art, etc.
- Closeout linens and bedding

JUNE

Once the majority of June weddings are over, graduations have passed, and Dad's Day is done, you'll find super deals on beautiful summer skirts, tops, and dresses. Gorgeous special-occasion items and girly, frilly things adorn the sale rack for as much as 50 percent off from June until the end of summer.

And believe it or not, swimsuits start to hit the sale rack in June. This might make you like shopping for them a bit more . . . but I doubt it! The latter half of June brings about the first round of summer price cuts, but keep in mind that the super-saving signs won't start sprouting until after July 4.

JULY

The Fourth of July fireworks signify more than just our country's birthday; they also celebrate one of my favorite things in the world: the resurrection of the 70 percent–off sign (yippee!). All things summer have to go after the Fourth! Stores have to clean out to make room for bulkier fall and winter items. Fall is historically the best retail season, and merchants are ready to bring it on! Fantastic sale rack finds can help you bridge your Cents of Style wardrobe into fall. This means July is the time to shop the sale rack for these items:

- That fabulous slinky dress for New Year's Eve
- Feminine day dresses and jumpers that can be worn under a winter blazer with boots and tights
- The perfect bathing suit for your winter cruise
- Summer's strappy, glamorous heels that will look stunning with your holiday ensembles
- Lace camis for sexy, peekaboo, body-skimming winter layers
- Cropped pants and Bermuda shorts in all-season fabrics to wear with fabulous fall boots
- Gold, copper, and bronze metallic accessories—sure to be classic for years to come
- Three-quarter-length jackets that will look urban and cool with longer sleeves peeking out.

AUGUST

Summer is still sweltering, but in August, thoughts turn to autumn. There is no doubt that this is *the* best time of year to shop. Back to school means parents and students are looking for deep discounts, and most retailers gleefully oblige. There are lots of bargains to be had as summer draws to a close and autumn springs eternal . . . or something like that.

Back-to-school bargains are a bonus for us all. Even if you're not hitting the books, you can still take advantage of fabulous back-to-school discounts at all of your favorite stores.

Students heading off to college need sheets, towels, paint, office furniture, bathroom supplies, organizational items, and computer equipment. They need jeans, sneakers, tees, underwear, bras, sweaters, jackets—you name it! If a student needs it, it's on sale in August.

Stores are clearing out summer items like shorts, tees, and tanks while at the same time pushing overstocked stu-

IF YOU'VE been contemplating redecorating a room, August is the time to do it. You'll find great buys on sheets, towels, paint, office furniture, computer equipment, and organizational items. Stores competitively try hard to lure budget-conscious parents and students, so you can ride the discount wave and do a little freshman nesting of your own.

dent basics piled high at every turn. No doubt, the yearly bargain-o-rama happens in August, so don't miss out on the opportunity to save!

Preseason sales also happen in August. Catalogs, flyers, and e-mail campaigns feature fall/winter items at a 15 to 25 percent discount if purchased before Labor Day. This retail trend is a blessing to all of us who wear common sizes that never seem to make it to the sale rack and those of us who simply don't have the patience to wait for things to go on sale. (I'm crying a little tear here!)

But whatever you do, don't purchase fall merchandise in August without asking or researching whether there is a discount that you were not aware of. It never hurts to inquire, and you just never know when that simple question will save you this week's gas money.

SEPTEMBER

Look for deep, deep discounts on spring and summer items in September. If an item hasn't left the stores yet, retailers are desperate to get rid of it. Holiday items are hitting their floors, and they need the room. Discounts of 70 to 85 percent are not uncommon for September sales.

I remember going bargain bananas at a September sale a few years ago, when the store was offering 75 percent off with an additional 30 percent off the sale price. I'm no mathematician, but I recall sweetly informing the salesclerk she could just give me a dollar to take the whole bag of clothes off her hands.

September is historically the biggest denim month of the year, and you can find jeans on sale everywhere. Jeans are America's uniform, and denim is the perfect fabric to bridge the seasons. And with summer gone, the demand for strapless, low-back, clear-strap, and halter bras folds like a beach umbrella. August and September are the time to go find one on the sale rack! You are sure to discover all of the bras that do summer tricks at a deep discount.

September's sale rack will be packed with these items:

- Overstock back-to-school items like denim, T-shirts, and activewear
- Convertible bras made for summer styles
- Sleepwear that will be just as cute and comfortable next year
- Housewares and party supplies designed for spring/summer that will make creative and thoughtful holiday gifts

OCTOBER

There aren't a lot of sales in the women's department in the month of October! This is the time of year, just like March, to go shopping for perspective. It won't be too long before items are discounted, but for most of October full-priced items are hanging on racks like grapes, so buyer beware.

Retailers know that we are all getting ready to host events for the holidays, so this month you will find great deals on all things entertaining, but not clothing items. Look for deep discounts on housewares, home goods, and culinary supplies. The stores always overstock, so if you can hold off till after Thanksgiving, you will find even larger savings.

Lots of new products are launched each fall as students return to class and households resume a regular routine of TV viewing and periodical reading. Advertisers simply get more bang for the buck in the autumn months. Many new products are offered at introductory pricing, which can mean huge saving for consumers. Keep your eyes peeled for big savings on all sorts of items—and if you like 'em, stock up!

MOST NATIONAL department stores will allow you to retroactively receive a discounted sale price for up to two weeks after purchase. It can't hurt to keep an eye out for falling prices and the receipt in your purse, especially for big-ticket items.

NOVEMBER

November is notorious for one thing in the retail world: the super bowl of all shopping days, also known as Black Friday, the day after Thanksgiving. It was dubbed Black Friday years ago, because this day pushes many retailers' balance sheets into the black ink for the year. What Black Friday promises is bargains, bargains as far as the eye can see. But Black Friday is not for the amateur shopper.

I always pick up the super-fat, ad-happy Thanksgiving Day edition of the local newspaper, gather around the dining room table with the dames in my family—after our turkey nap, of course—and map out what stores we want to hit first. Yep, when it comes to Black Friday, a true strategy is required!

Many stores offer early-morning deals in limited quantities, so "camping out" to save a bundle can offer hilarious bonding fun for you and your family and/or girlfriends. I can remember my Aunt Ann and me staying up all night one year to get a super deal at a local store. We laughed and joked, plotting our mission like cunning hunters in the woods. That early morning, we bagged a computer at an insane price, and we still get tickled at how much fun we had.

Here are a few tips on how to make the most of the most glorious of all shopping days, Black Friday:

- Comb the Thanksgiving Day newspaper for all of the big sales.

- Gather all of the ads for the items you wish to buy. This will serve as proof, if you get to the store and they tell you the item is not on sale or if you want another store to match the advertised price of an item.

- Create a priority list of the most-wanted and least-expensive items.

- Have a budget of what you can spend, and stick to it.

- Plan on getting up super early and having breakfast before you head out. Stopping to eat is not an option; have PowerBars and bottled water at the ready!

- Wear comfortable shoes and light clothing. The stores get packed with people, and it gets hot. You then end up lugging your coat or sweater for the rest of the day.

- Once you hit the stores, do not be lured away from finding your must-have items first. When you have those in tow, you can look through other things that catch your interest. Stay focused on your list!

- If you are shopping at a mall, organize a handoff time with a friend or relative. You can hand off many of your purchases to someone who will drive them back home while you continue to shop. This is extremely helpful. Shopping when you are loaded down is exhausting, and taking the packages to your car is a pain and can be unsafe. You will be amazed at how freeing this can be and how much more you can get done.

DECEMBER

Among my favorite things to pop up on sale tables during December are gift sets or kits—you know, those great miniature collection cosmetic kits, grooming kits, stationery kits, tool kits, travel kits, etc. These strategically small and perfectly planned collections disappear when the tinsel comes down. They are never around in May when you need such genius groupings for that only-one-suitcase-allowed road trip.

So when you stumble upon that brilliant make-your-life-easier bargain gift kit, pick up one for yourself, and store it in your luggage. You will love the surprise when you pull down that bag come spring. Genius!

If you've made it to December, holding out for that special winter purchase, keep holding just a couple more days. Come December 26, all of your sale rack fantasies come true! (In my sale rack fantasy, Harry Connick Jr. follows me around, carrying my bags of thrifty-chic loot, all purchased from my favorite stores at a minimum of 50 percent off. Woo-hoo!) Though Harry might not be around, the week after Christmas signals major markdowns on great cold-weather items. So get your gift cards ready, and go get 'em!

Stumbling upon a great deal is fun, but preparing for it is where the real bargain glee comes in. Following this cunning retail calendar will ensure that you are always prepared to spend less. No surprises—you know you can get great deals on bras in February, dresses in June, jeans in August, and boots in January. With this calendar tip sheet, you can save up to get the best deals on things you really want, watch your mail for additional savings coupons you can apply to big-ticket items, and/or drop some hints that diamonds are on huge sale at the end of May. *(Wink!)*

The Power of Color and Creativity

8

A TRUE VALUE VIXEN understands the undeniable fashion force of color. It is the most magnificently thrifty style tool we have, but for many of us it is also the most underutilized. The thoughtful use of rich, stunning color has magical transforming powers to slim, emphasize, radiate, and beautify your body. Color is a wardrobe wonder weapon that every gal should know how to wield. So poke your head out of the black fashion cloud for a bit, and let's think about a little pigmented pick-me-up. No more blah blah black sheep—it's time for a ray of sunshine and a pop of color!

THE PSYCHOLOGY OF COLOR

Color is an incredible fashion tool that's often taken for granted. We are all naturally attracted to color, and it stimulates emotional, physical, and even behavioral responses. We don't just notice colors; we actually feel them, and they can not only reflect our moods, but often alter them as well. Every fashion decision we make has a color connection that sends a message to others and reflects our personality. Choosing colors wisely can work to your advantage and help elevate your style game.

Most importantly for thrifty divas, great color has a perceived worth. Certain colors simply look more sophisticated and stylish, so choosing those colors can boost the look of a budget garment without adding a dime to the price tag. Understanding what message the color is sending is the key, so once again, we can make better choices and look like a million without spending a fortune. (Can I get an *Amen*?)

The science behind color reveals that we interpret certain colors to mean specific things. A stunning purple blouse reflects a passionate visionary. To-die-for red shoes communicate energy, determination, and charisma. Your chocolate-brown suit tells your boss you are stable, earthy, and reliable. The beautiful turquoise scarf you never wear could be telling the world you are motivated, active, and dynamic, and the fantastic yellow handbag that you were so attracted to before you opted to go with the black instead would have declared you optimistic, playful, and enthusiastic. Quite simply, color is an electrifying wardrobe device that carries great power yet doesn't have to cost an extra penny.

TIPS

HERE ARE a few of the colorful messages you're sending when you choose a beautiful color:

- **RED** represents joy, sexuality, passion, sensitivity, confidence, and love.

- **PINK** signifies romance, love, and friendship. It denotes feminine qualities and passiveness.
- **DARK RED** is associated with vigor, willpower, leadership, and courage.
- **BROWN** suggests stability, reliability, and earthiness.
- **REDDISH BROWN** is associated with harvest and fall, meaning abundance and warmth.
- **RED-ORANGE** corresponds to desire, sexual passion, pleasure, domination, and thirst for action.
- **GOLD** evokes the feeling of prestige. The meaning of gold is illumination, wisdom, and wealth.
- **YELLOW** is associated with intellect, freshness, optimism, playfulness, and joy.
- **DARK GREEN** is associated with ambition and drive.
- **AQUA** is associated with emotional healing as well as protection.
- **TURQUOISE** says you are motivated, active, and dynamic.
- **OLIVE GREEN** is the traditional color of peace.
- **BLUE** is associated with health, healing, tranquility, and understanding.
- **DARK BLUE** represents knowledge, power, integrity, and seriousness.
- **LIGHT PURPLE** evokes romantic and nostalgic feelings.
- **DEEP PURPLE** is the color of royalty, representing passion, great vision, and imagination.
- **BLACK** is associated with power, formality, death, evil, and mystery.
- **WHITE** is associated with light, goodness, innocence, purity, and virginity.

The one constant in all colors that evoke strong feelings and responses is vibrancy. Think about Jada Pinkett Smith on the red carpet in that rich canary-yellow gown at the Oscars, America Ferrara accepting her Emmy (Best Actress in a Comedy Series: “Ugly Betty”) in gorgeous royal blue, or Oprah in that amazing lipstick-red dress at her famous Legends Ball. Pale yellow or tints of ice just don’t convey your fashion moxie the same way gorgeous jewel tones do, and they certainly don’t maximize your wardrobe dollars.

Pale colors rarely do anything for your skin tone and usually are perceived as a little mousy. Richer colors like peacock blue, fuchsia, pumpkin, emerald green, and deep purple send a strong, confident message. Distinctive, saturated color is an important tool for building an empowered, thrifty-chic wardrobe. So buy those fabulous green boots on the sale rack, the tangerine sweater that is 70 percent off, or that amazing indigo handbag instead of the black, and wear it like you mean it!

Deliberately use colorful pieces as your style statements. If you are a girl who is most comfortable swaddled in black, show your adventurous side with a chartreuse handbag,

TIPS

A GREAT way to perk up an old coat and a cold winter’s day is with a new scarf, hat, and gloves in a bright, vibrant color. After the holidays, winter woollies hit the sale rack, and this is the perfect time to refresh your outer layers so you won’t get sick of them till spring. But go bold; choose a color you would have never thought of. This is a great way to be affordably adventurous.

bold jade earrings, or a stack of colorful bangles. If you live in a gray fog and frolic in tones of stone, charcoal, and slate, make your unique style statement with a fuchsia wrap, sea-green coat, or cognac boots. You will step higher, feel better, and catch the eyes as you pass by. Your confident, colorful fashion message will convey a pretty penny, even if you didn't spend one . . . Hey, there goes that spunky, fun girl with the super-cool style!

STRATEGIC USE OF COLOR

As you know, your Cents of Style wardrobe is built on a figure-enhancing workforce of earth-toned anchor pieces and colorful tops and accessories. This is the most economical way to build your wardrobe, but it's also the most flattering. By keeping your beautifully tailored anchor pieces dark, neutral, and adornment free, you are creating a feminine structural frame. This frame then works to set off the colors you add to the ensemble and allows you to pull focus up to your beautiful face, skin, hair, and eyes.

The colorful tops and accessories you apply to your dark anchor pieces capture the attention, highlight your upper body, deemphasize your lower half, and naturally make you look taller and leaner. This is also known as fashion color blocking, strategically using light and dark colors to minimize figure flaws and showcase the good stuff.

To round out a tactical color block, you want to follow through with the color of your anchor pieces all the way down to your legs and shoes. For example, if you have on a black skirt, you would add black opaque tights and black shoes or boots; chocolate trousers would call for brown trouser socks and brown shoes. The point is to create an uninterrupted dark block of color on your bottom half that will simply support the vibrant highlight color worn on top.

Now that you know this little fashion trick, you may notice that fashion color blocking is used a lot on television. As a stylist, working with a variety of different people, I recognize that the eye naturally follows color, so I have cleverly used this strategy on many of my makeovers for television, as well as on celebrity clients shooting commercials and being interviewed on talk shows. Fashion color blocking is easy, and it really works!

COLOR BLOCKING is a beautiful and effective style approach for ladies wanting to minimize their tummies and booties, especially in photos.

As I mentioned before, color has implied value and can tactfully elevate the look of a very inexpensive garment. If a top is offered in five colors—say, pale pink, cream, red, black, and teal—the teal is going to look much more expensive than the other shades, because it's a *richer* color. A thrifty teal tank will add instant sophistication and luxury to an otherwise inexpensive outfit, simply because it is a sophisticated color. So a fabulous thrifty diva should always choose the richest, most saturated, and unique colors when shopping for tops and accessories on the sale rack. A cheap, rich color is the ultimate style irony and oh, so thrifty chic.

BANG-FOR-YOUR-BUCK HUES	BLAH COLORS
DO choose . . .	**DON'T waste your $$ on . . .**
Peacock blue	Light blue
Sunflower yellow	Sickly yellow-green
Emerald green	Mousy dull green
Lipstick red	Pale, fleshy pink
Pumpkin orange	Washed-out peach
Cognac brown	Light tan
Amazing vivid color	Flesh tones

MAN-CATCHING COLOR

Now how 'bout a hue to hail the fellahs? Well, studies have shown that men like solid colors over patterns and are most attracted to a woman in a sugary coral tone. This deep, vibrant pink-peach color makes you more approachable, flatters your skin, and makes your lips and cheeks look rosy, giving you a healthy glow, according to color consultant Leatrice Eiseman, director of the Pantone Color Institute and author of *Colors for Your Every Mood*. Pinky hues also project a little vulnerability, which brings out the gallant, protective, masculine side of a man. Who doesn't love and want that stuff?

Red is a very sensual color that conveys a confident message, but it also represents sex and power to most men. So if you're on the prowl for a man-mate, wearing red will attract two kinds of dudes—those who are interested in a little mattress mambo and those who can't get enough of powerful dames! That red dress will mean you have to weed through a few freaks, but you may just find a soul mate eager to help you run for president.

On the other side of things, you, my dear, will find yourself most attracted to men who wear a lot of blue. Eiseman claims that guys who fill their closet with a sea of blue are "stable, faithful, constant, and always there." The blue guy will prove to be dependable and monogamous—and can probably match his clothes, because blue goes with almost everything. Blue guy could also easily become long-term-relationship guy.

If you are looking to repel folks, male or female, pile on the puke green. The yucky yellow-green color that reminds us of something sick actually does make your peeps a little queasy. Studies show that this color is the least liked by both sexes, so for goodness' sake, don't buy it or sport it to your next job interview.

CENTS OF STYLE COLOR FORMULA

Another great color strategy—what I like to call my Cents of Style Color Formula—offers a high-style impact for no additional budget bucks. The formula is to use complementary colors with your tops and accessories. Complementary colors sit opposite each other on the color wheel, so they look especially lively when paired. When you put complementary colors together, each color becomes more noticeable.

A simpler way of approaching this is to think in terms of cool tones, or colors of water (blues, greens, purples, and lavenders), and warm tones, or colors of fire (reds, yellows, oranges, and pinks). When your top is a cool tone, choose warm-toned accessories, and when your top is a warm tone, choose cool-toned accessories. For example, if you have on a rich brick-red blouse with charcoal-gray anchor pieces, adding turquoise earrings or a jade pendant necklace offers a juxtaposition that creates visual intrigue and fashion finesse. Adding gray, silver, or black accessories to the ensemble would be OK but certainly wouldn't offer the unexpected style punch of accessories in complementary colors.

If you are wearing a beautiful patterned dress consisting of vibrant blue, black, and white, pair it with yellow bangles and earrings or perhaps red shoes and a red handbag; either group would offer an unexpected stylish twist. The complementary-color accessories will highlight the blue in the dress and make the entire outfit seem more spectacular and electrified. Whatever you do, don't play up the black in the dress with simple black, white, or metallic accessories; you want to make the blue pop.

A great example of the Cents of Style Color Formula at work is that wonderful image of Cameron Diaz at the Oscars in 2002. Cameron wore an exotic blush-colored dress with large flowers in tones of burgundy, red, pumpkin, and grape all over it. The stunning style twist that had everyone abuzz was the incredible chunky turquoise bracelet that she paired with it. The turquoise made the other colors sing and elevated the outfit into another style realm.

So do you get it? Just remember to accessorize your outfit with the opposite color family of the predominant color you are wearing. Even if you are wearing a pattern, gauge what the standout color is, and complement it with opposing colors. This color formula is very easy to follow and will always render you fashion forward. This could be a big fashion risk for you in the beginning, but I know you can do it. And the comments of how great you look, how creative you've become, and "Oh! Did you get a makeover?"—there'll be so much sugar coming your way, you're gonna think it's raining gumdrops and lollipops.

WHAT COLORS LOOK BEST ON YOU?

Richer, more vibrant, crisp colors look beautiful on everyone. Saturated hues bring life to your face, skin tone, and hair and can pull focus to your eyes. Most eyes, even dark eyes like mine, have many beautiful flecks of color in them, so choosing to wear shades that either reflect or highlight the colors in your eyes is a very powerful fashion move. By wearing colors that showcase your eyes, you are subliminally encouraging people to visually bathe in your peepers, which will help build connection and trust. It also enhances overall attraction from others (and who doesn't mind that?).

When choosing tops, jackets, and other things that are worn close to your face, you can wear any *color* you like; ultimately it's the shade that is going to make the difference. High pigment tones, colors that are deeper and more dynamic, simply carry more power and reflect more confidence. Brilliant, lively colors like candy-apple red, cobalt blue, and hot magenta are magnetic and indicate a stronger sense of fashion, creativity, and courage. Additionally, beautiful colors make you feel beautiful; they spark energy and stimulate positive feelings.

It's always best to stay away from light noncolors like beiges and wheat tones, which do nothing to enhance your complexion, eyes, or hair. Black is equally bad when worn next to the face, because it deadens your skin tone and makes you look older by exaggerating any dark areas or lines on your face. Considering this, it's shocking to think that in a recent poll on my website (centsofstyle.com), almost 90 percent of women said they incorporate black into their wardrobe a minimum of once a week; most opt for black more than twice a week. So let's talk about why black is so appealing to so many and how to wear it more "centsibly."

WHEN GIVEN the option of a black or brown garment, remember that brown will always look richer and wear better. The more you wash and wear brown, the more rugged and natural it looks. But the more you wash and wear black, the more gray and used it looks!

Black is considered a very sophisticated color that goes with everything, doesn't show dirt, and makes us look thinner. All of these things can be true, but we need to be careful not to fall into a black fashion hole. Wearing black all the time is too predictable, and it slowly saps your fashion mojo. You gotta add some color, life, and richness to your thrifty-chic threads.

Truth is, darker colors naturally absorb the light and, as a result, do help make us look thinner. Keep in mind, this goes for all dark colors, such as chocolate brown, navy blue, and charcoal gray. All of these tones work in the same way that black does to camouflage and deflect the eye, but they offer a richer variance.

It's also important to remember that it's the *fit* of a garment that will make you look taller, slimmer, and shapelier, not the color. A perfectly fitted white suit will look a thousand times more slimming on a full-figured frame than a black suit that hangs, pulls, and gathers in all the wrong places. The key to camouflage is finding your perfect fit and then using color to flatter your eyes, skin, and hair and pull attention to your assets. Color catches our eye and makes us look terrific, and it usually costs the same as the black blouse you picked up to buy, so don't get stuck in a black fashion rut. Turn up your fashion wattage with color, and shine on!

COLOR COURAGE

Though we are all attracted to color, tend to have a favorite color, and would agree that some colors simply make us feel great, most of us have closets that are, well, colorless! Committing to color can be very hard for some people, because they don't want to make a fashion mistake, and sometimes it's just easier to have fewer choices. Wearing noncolors or the same neutral colors all of the time (not out of necessity, like a work requirement) is a reflection of fear, fashion indecision, and a lack of creativity. But you don't have to live in *Pleasantville.* We can all enjoy a colorful life and closet. The power of color is one that everyone can easily harness with one simple choice: turquoise or coral?

The colors turquoise and coral are the two most powerful colors on the color wheel, because each of them incorporates every color in their tone family. Turquoise represents all of the cool tones, and coral represents all of the warm tones. As a result, there is nothing that won't complement or coordinate with either of these colors, and they look great on everyone. Remember, the fellahs like a pink-peach *coral* color!

Wearing turquoise or coral offers high-impact, skin-flattering, positive results that you will hear about all day long. If you currently have these colors in your closet, I am sure you know what I mean. Whenever you wear them, people constantly compliment you, and you seem more energized and tend to attract people to you in a different way. I'd even be willing to bet you consider your turquoise or coral garments lucky. That's the power of color.

Both colors offer the perfect diving board into the color pool. As you begin to add more color to your wardrobe, they will continue to look great with all of your new additions. Once you have committed to either turquoise or coral, continuing to build in the same color family is the next step. If turquoise is your color, then adding new tops and jackets in other cool tones will help maintain a coordinating thread and make it easier to add impactful complementary accessories. If coral is your first step of color courage, continue to add warm-toned tops and jackets, and don't forget to gather cool-toned accessories to make it all pop with panache.

HOW TO BE MORE CREATIVE IN YOUR DRESSING

Becoming more stylish and creative in your dressing can be tough. It requires one very bold and confident move that many women find difficult to do because of self-set social boundaries and/or judgments. This one act often takes coaxing, prodding, and weeks of encouragement to get ladies to relax and prepare. It seems so very simple, yet at times it is the most difficult task imaginable—so do you know what it is? *Honor your likes!* Yep, you will find your personal, creative, fashion bliss when you simply honor what you like and are attracted to.

So many of us are attracted to color, yet our entire wardrobe is black. We love a pretty dress but talk ourselves out of buying one because we have no place to wear it. We're dying to sport fabulous strappy sandals, but Greg Murphy told us we had ugly feet in the sixth grade, so we keep our tootsies covered. We'd feel like a rock star in leather, but what would the neighbors say if I wore a leather skirt?

All of these limitations and self-imposed restrictions stunt our creative growth and keep us from actualizing the style goddess within. Now, I am not saying that you should start dressing in "character" or take things to a costume-like extreme, but what I am encouraging you to do is to start incorporating unexpected atypical items into your wardrobe that reflect your spunk and sparkle—even if it is just with color.

If you love the color green, buy a fabulously thrifty green leather watch, and wear it with everything. Each time you check your watch, you will be reminded of your color courage and willingness to honor your likes. No doubt, you will receive a jamillion compliments on your fantastic green watch, and you will be encouraged to make more creative and stylish efforts with your wardrobe.

Say you love girly day dresses, but wearing them makes you feel overdressed and uncomfortable. Go ahead and buy that dress you love, and play it down with casual accessories like flat shoes or sandals, a canvas handbag, and costume jewelry versus the real stuff, and maybe top it with a denim blazer. This will visually cast a comfortable, relaxed feel to your favorite new dress and keep you at ease with both your fashion fabulosity and your confident, creative style.

With every fashion risk that honors who you are, you will assuredly get feedback, usually positive, which will strengthen your style muscles and encourage you to travel your own creative path. You simply need the courage to respect your fashion essence and wear what makes you feel happy. By tastefully and strategically following your happiness, you will develop an individual flair and personal Cents of Style. This seems like a simple step, but I know it can be very hard. Push yourself. Life is too short not to wear red shoes!

HOW TO CREATE YOUR OWN STYLE

A signature piece, a color that you are known for, a fashion era that you emulate, a cultural flair you incorporate, or a distinctive way you coordinate—all of these are characteristics of personal style. When someone comments that she saw something while shopping that reminded her of you, congratulations! You have your own personal style.

Developing a unique, enviable fashion flair doesn't have to be hard. In fact, it may be much easier than developing color courage or taking risks with your likes. By simply committing to a theme or a style mantra, a focus regarding your wardrobe, you can quickly and effectively establish your own personal style. I encourage this from my clients all of the time as we set out to build a wardrobe that sends a visual message and communicates who they are, where they've been, and where they are headed.

A fashion goal such as casual glamour, tough femininity, ethnic sophistication, or retro modernity can keep you directed down a particular shopping path, helping guide selections and assembly of your masterful thrifty-chic wardrobe. Setting a specific intention will clarify your fashion message, and soon you will start to develop a fabulous personal style.

When I think of the mantra of casual glamour, Gwen Stefani immediately comes to mind. Ms. Stefani looks amazing in anything, but no matter how casual and modern she is, she is all glamour from the neck up. She always wears crimson-red lipstick, oversized Hollywood sunglasses, and a modern blond coif, even in cargo shorts and a tank. Now I am not suggesting you go to this extreme, but this is an example of an incredible style icon who lives by the fashion mantra of casual easy glamour. You can do that, too.

A recent poll asked subscribers to my E-nnouncements (my e-mail newsletter at centsofstyle.com) what they most like to shop for. Well, a surprising 10 percent of responders said they hate shopping completely, finding it frustrating and annoying. (Insert my sad face here, though I understand your pain!) But 27 percent said they love shopping for all things girl-tastic—going about it with gusto and a thrifty-diva spirit, no doubt. (Smile returns.) The rest of them fell somewhere in between, reveling in the hunt for specific items such as jeans, shoes, dresses, cosmetics, and accessories.

The lesson to be learned here is that shopping for what you like and staying true to your creative fashion spirit helps you develop your own personal style. Quite simply, gather and wear what you love! Think about the message that you want to send to the world, and live it through your image. And if you don't absolutely love something, don't buy it! That sounds so simple, but we all buy things we really don't like.

If you love shoes, then by all means make them your style statement. Become known as the girl with the cutest shoes on the block. If dresses float your boat, find more ways to incorporate them into your weekly wardrobe; don't just save them for special occasions. If you dig being in casual clothes, opt for an upscale casual look that blends both business and casual attire, like fitted hoodies with pencil skirts, casual tees under business suits, or jeans and classic blazers.

Take stock of what fashion items put a spring in your step and ignite conversations with friends and strangers. The items you love are the things that herald your spirit, so don't make wimpy choices. Go for it! By showcasing just one sweet fashion gem, you are sending a confident message that will overshadow the fact that you're not quite as happy with the rest of your outfit (but we are working on that, right?).

Just remember, developing your own style is all about skylarking in your loves and making a unique fashion statement with them. Using the Cents of Style Color Formula will go a long way in helping you, and it's easy—just choose opposing tones for your tops and accessories. Your flair for the unexpected and joy from wearing things you love will surely give you a great Cents of Style!

Accessorize, Accessorize, Accessorize

9

I ABSOLUTELY LOVE ACCESSORIES because of their amazing fashion power! Accessories set the tone, paint the picture, and help shape your image. Accessories are the quickest and most inexpensive way to update and optimize your wardrobe. Like little stylish signals, they flash your intentions, your creative essence, and your sense of modernity.

The right accessories can make that basic black A-line skirt (cut to the knee, please!) sing at the opera or beat a steel drum at a pool party. Accessories can transform your basic jeans and T-shirt into modern, polished glamour-girl perfection in seconds flat. These little transitioning tools are your creative palette, and your flawless, figure-flattering wardrobe workforce is the canvas on which you can devise your divalicious Cents of Style image.

Accessories set the mood of an outfit, offering polish and panache. One of my favorite things about accessories is that, for the most part, they don't come in a size. (Woo-hoo!) Your earrings don't care how big your booty is, yet your earrings can herald your fanciful spirit and urban edge. No matter what the scale says, a hot pair of sunglasses seems to put some motion in your ocean and make your lips perfectly purse with attitude.

Accessories have the incredible power to make us look both *hip* and, remarkably, less *hip-py* as they showcase the most feminine parts of us, pulling attention away from figure flaws. Accessories bring focus to our décolleté and neck, showcase our tiny wrists, create shape through the waist, and play up our beautiful, lash-batting eyes. Trust me, no one will notice the telltale signs of your weeklong boyfriend-breakup Ben & Jerry's binge if you wow them with a gorgeous pair of teardrop earrings; bold, colorful watch; hot, modern handbag; and sinfully cute shoes (Amen!).

Another wonderful thing about accessories, just like clothing styles, is that they always regenerate, and if you take care of them, you can hand them down from generation to generation. I am so, *so* fortunate to have been the recipient of much of my Big-Mammaw Hearn's (that's great-grandma where I come from) and my Great-Aunt Mildred's costume jewelry. I cherish the incredible pieces that they left me, and when I wear them, I think of how chic and stylish they must have been, what hot chicks they probably were in their day, and how proud I am to wear what they loved and wore.

I believe you should never throw away good accessories. If you take care of your accessories and they remain in good condition, you can wear them for years, each time they come back in style. Or better yet, hand them down to younger thrifty divas and shopper heroes in your life who will love being creative with your stylish stuff.

Accessories also hold a lot of social power. If you notice, rarely does someone compliment you on your pants or your wardrobe workforce, because those are the silent strength of your image. What people notice and respond to are your accessories and the colors your wear. A killer necklace will launch a hundred conversations, bold and creative eyeglasses can make you more approachable, and a modern handbag with smokin' shoes could get you friendlier service at your favorite stores.

Accessories hold all the potential of that stylish starlet that lives within us. You just need to wake up and reach for a scarf. When it comes to making bold fashion moves, you don't want to take that risk with your britches, so buy a bold accessory instead. This is a great way to start building your color courage and offer more expressive and fashionable visual interest to your image without breaking the bank.

FINDING AND BUYING ACCESSORIES FOR LESS

You do want to apply the same Cents of Style budget-shopping techniques when shopping for accessories. You always look for the sale area first. You never know what you will find. But shopping for accessories is much easier than shopping for clothes, because we don't have to head to the fitting room to try them on, and they are usually displayed in such a way that we can easily identify what has our name on it. Bargain accessories are never a bad investment, because they do your style talkin'. Trendy items are simple additions that easily sew up a stylish look and make a major impact on your fashion wattage.

I'm here to tell you right now that one of the best places to find great inexpensive accessories is in thrift stores. The accessories in most thrift stores are prominently displayed and don't require a full-on dig to uncover. You can easily peruse the handbags, scarves, earrings, bracelets, and the like in minutes flat, and the bargains are, of course, incredible. The goal of thrift store accessory shopping is not to find the items that are hot and current at the moment, but to look for the items that are well preserved, in perfect condition, and look like ten times the price.

Just because an accessory is in a thrift store and is not in style right now doesn't mean it should be passed up. Several years ago, I purchased a dozen or more perfectly strung glass beads in all different colors and designs at a thrift store in Fort Wayne, Indiana. These beautiful long beads were certainly too bold for the minimal-accessory trend of the early nineties, but I held onto them and layered them like a rock star a few seasons back, when beads popped back on fashion runways like a Whack-a-Mole.

Remember, thrift stores carry donated items that have not been cleaned, so you will want to wash, dry-clean, or disinfect whatever you purchase. (But to be honest, it is not a bad idea to clean almost anything you buy.)

Ethnic neighborhoods, as explained in Chapter 6, and areas of the country where specific fashion styles are prevalent and plentiful are other incredible resources for unique, inexpensive items that offer a great amount of style for not a lot of moola! Picking up a beautiful silver cuff bracelet while you are in El Paso, jade earrings while shopping in Chinatown, or fabulous cowboy boots at a truck stop in

Wyoming are perfect examples of thinking like a shopper hero.

I confess that I bought my favorite cognac-colored leather belt with simple buffed-brass details for five dollars at a truck stop in Montgomery, Alabama. I have worn this belt with jeans for more than ten years and continue to get compliments on it. I certainly didn't head to the truck stop looking for a fashion find, but my eyes were open when I went in, saw this incredible collection of Western wear, and made a detour on my way to the potty. I'll be darned if my five-dollar truck stop belt doesn't look like a Ralph Lauren creation—and nobody's the wiser.

Another thing to remember about accessories is that they offer a creative and stylish opportunity to do a bit more experimenting. I could have bought a black belt at my truck stop, but I liked the look of that five-dollar cognac belt. I didn't have any particular outfit in mind when I bought it, but the color was rich, and it offered more visual interest with its simple thick brass buckle, so I was willing to take the chance. (And for five dollars, you can afford to take that chance!) That is exactly how you should assess accessories: as an expression of what you like.

WORKIN' IT!

Go for the unexpected! Choose things that catch your eye and, again, that reflect your likes. Accessories aren't your wardrobe workforce, so you don't have to visualize three different ways you can wear them. Simply choose items you are attracted to, and then creatively incorporate them into your wardrobe. Accessories are creative tools, and you can never have too many. Plus the more you like it, the more you'll want to wear it, and the easier it will be to showcase it with your wardrobe.

No matter the season, think about mixing unexpected colors and unifying your look with a unique, beloved accessory that surprisingly works to pull the whole outfit together. Clever fashion concoctions with a keen use of accessories are exactly how you look like a million without spending a fortune. Putting things together with your own flavor is the fun of getting dressed.

Now let's look at all the great, fun fashion accessories you can use to your Cents of Style advantage.

SHOOOOOOES!

There is no hiding the fact that I love shoes! I have worn the same shoe size since I was ten years old, so I boast a righteous, well-preserved, thrifty-chic collection. I am one of those chicks who is willing to endure the pain of uncomfortable shoes for the sake of a perfectly styled outfit—all for under a hundred bucks of course. But I am certainly not suggesting you go to this fashion extreme. We gals have places to go, people to meet, and worlds to conquer, and if our feet hurt, our whole body hurts. That's why good shoe picking is important stuff.

The right shoes can make or break any outfit. They really dictate the mood of an ensemble. One of the fastest ways to change your look is to change your shoes. Jeans and a delicate tank top can go from doing laundry in the basement to doing the boogie-woogie on a dance floor with a quick change out of your sneakers and into hot, strappy heels. No doubt, changing those sneakers also changes your attitude.

Let's face it—we tend to show our respect, confidence, and feminine intentions for an event by how high we are willing to lift our heels off the floor. Grocery shopping gets flats, but special nights out get come-hither pumps! We all have that special pair of shoes in our closet that may very well kill our feet, but we feel so sexy in them, we are willing to take stunted, geisha-like steps from the car to the closest chair we can find at the party and back to the car when the shindig's all done!

Because shoes serve such specific functions in our lives, many of us, no matter how advanced a shopper hero, live by the dictum that we have to sacrifice comfort for style and, worse, style for comfort. This is simply *not* the case. Cute, comfy, confidence-boosting shoes can be found at great prices. You just have to dedicate yourself to the hunt (but it's worth it).

Bad, manly-looking clodhoppers are not empowering. In fact, it is the exact opposite: ugly shoes are like a diva drain. When you put them on, your fashion mojo leaks out of your feet. Taking the time to find spunky, comfortable kickers is *mucho* important for maintaining your "look like a million" attitude.

IF THE shoe fits, wear it! Shoes, just like garments, end up on the sale rack due to sizing issues. Be sure to look at the sale shoes a half size larger and smaller than your size to ensure you're not missing a major bargain.

Understanding what is going to look best on your foot, what heel type is going to slim your leg, and generally how to find a shoe that will look fabulous and not torture your lower back is the trifecta of shoe-shopping know-how. Throw in some Cents of Style shopping strategies to bag your shoes at rock-bottom prices, and you'll be high stepping in some super-cute shoes. In this day and age, there is simply *no* excuse for wearing horrible man shoes. Here are a few things to remember when shopping. Frumpy shoes, be gone!

Shoe Rules

- Dress up an outfit with your shoes.
- The same old shoe style that you love can be made fun and fresh if you choose an unexpected color. There is a reason songs are written about blue suede shoes; color packs a fashion punch.
- Choose shoes with sculpted, contoured, *feminine* heels. The chunkier the heel, the chunkier your legs look, and the more masculine the shoe.
- Shoes that are cut lower across the foot and show a little toe cleavage create long, lovely legs. The farther up on your foot that a shoe comes, the shorter your legs look.
- Avoid high-contrast ankle straps! If you are light skinned, no dark ankle straps, and my dark-skinned lovelies should avoid light-colored ankle straps. You want a clean unbroken line from the base of your shoe all the way up your leg; this makes your legs look longer and your ankles look slimmer.
- Watch your toes. Shoes with square or round toes can appear very masculine. An almond-shaped toe or a

pointed toe makes your legs look longer and will always appear more feminine.

- Wedge heels are a great, modern option that offer height and comfort while walking. A wedge heel absorbs the shock to your joints and proves a comfy boost in height and confidence.
- Avoid thick, straight straps across the top of your foot. These will make your legs look larger and your feet look wider.

Remember, consignment shops are great places to find fabulous shoes at great prices. Shoes that hurt someone's tootsies after one or two wearings can't be returned to a store, so they quite often end up on the rack of a fabulous consignment boutique. Hey, just because they hurt one set of toes doesn't mean they'll hurt yours, and shoes on consignment have hardly been worn. Check the bottom of the shoes to gauge the newness. I'll bet you'll be surprised.

All of your Cents of Style shopping strategies should certainly apply to the shoe department. Use your Cents of Style retail calendar to know the best time to shop, go to the sale rack first when entering the shoe department, shop end-of-the-season bargains, look for shoes one size larger and one size smaller than your normal size, consider a rich unexpected color, and, when applicable, buy the best leather you can afford, as leather shoes can be resoled and ultimately last longer.

Remember, cute shoes are one of the five keys to looking fabulous every day, and ugly shoes are fashion kryptonite! Don't be sapped of your shopper-hero power. With just a little savvy know-how and a courageous push to try new styles and colors you haven't before, you'll be high-steppin' in awesomely yummy shoes.

THE PERFECT HANDBAG FOR YOU

In case you haven't heard, size matters—especially when it comes to your handbag! Believe it or not, the right handbag can make you look taller, leaner, shapelier, and more modern and confident, while the wrong handbag can make you look stumpy and sloppy, give you a big butt, and generally make you look larger than you are. Your purse is powerful.

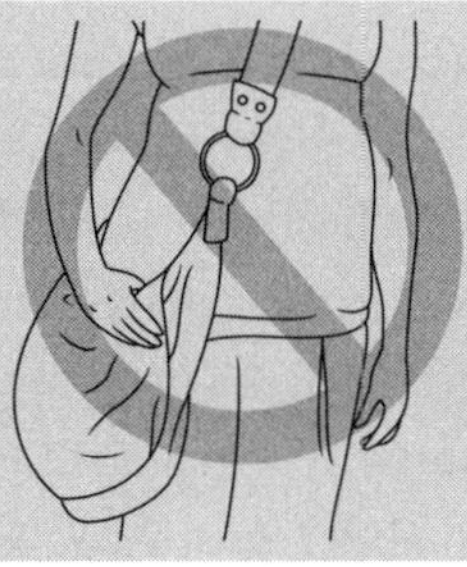

PURSES THAT hang down around your hip visually add girth to that area and make you look shorter and fuller in the seat.

Not only does the size matter, but your purse is also your social barometer. It tells the world who you are, where you are going, and what kind of stuff you need when you get there. In the past decade, handbags have taken center stage in the accessory show as Hollywood A-listers have helped elevate good ol' fashion purse toting to a high-stakes game of fashion battleship. With the hottest styles having year-long wait lists and the average price of a designer handbag

FANNY PACKS are not your friend! The term alone should be an indicator, but in case you are hesitant to cast off these waist bags, let me be clearer. When worn in the back, they add junk to your trunk, and when worn in the front, they add pounds to your pooch.

doubling and even quadrupling over the past few years, it is quite obvious that the *right* stuff holder means something.

The recent phenomenal emphasis placed on handbags has seen miraculous improvements in the technology of faux leathers. Amazing textures and dedication to details can be found in all styles of inexpensive handbags, and as a result, enjoying a handbag wardrobe is much easier than it used to be. Sporting a replica of a Queen Elizabeth–style top-handle bag, a Nicole Richie oversized hobo, or a Sharon Stone–like tote are all possible and super affordable. The replica market is huge because, as you learned in Chapter 6, you can't patent a design. So finding your favorite styles at inexpensive price points is easy; you just have to shop with a discriminating eye.

Now, keep in mind that while a fabulous thrifty diva wants to allude to hot designer currentness, she should never wear a fake bag with a designer's name or logo splashed all over it. My philosophy on this has always been that if designers want me to advertise their company, they should pay me—I shouldn't pay them. We are not billboards, ladies.

Our fashion choices should speak of *our own* creativity, not someone else's.

You can make a strong style statement with a structured handbag in a rich color. In fact, when you are trying to push yourself out of the black fashion hole, this is exactly where you want to start. The strategic use of rich colors in your handbags offers an immediate style boost.

A great way to think about your handbag is that it's like wearable, functional art. You want it to offer visual interest, reflect your creative spirit, and stimulate your senses. The point is to say no to the dreaded basic black box with a handle and recognize the potential of this important accessory. Don't forfeit the opportunity to be unforgettably fashionable. When choosing a handbag, follow these simple tips:

- Choose medium-sized styles proportioned to your height. Tiny handbags make you look larger, and a huge oversized bag can make you look like you're carrying luggage.
- Handbags should be worn in the bend of your waist and not slung low at your hip. A handbag that fits under your arm and sits at the bend of your waist makes you look taller and more shapely.
- Richer colors look richer. Don't wimp out on me. You'll be glad you ditched the black.

DANGLES, BAUBLES, BEADS, AND BRACELETS

Fashion or costume jewelry is the spice in your style stew. It's impossible to pull off a tasty look without it. The right earrings, necklace, brooch, watch, or bracelet can add the final touch of polish that sells your Cents of Style outfit as a much pricier ensemble.

One of my favorite Cents of Style accessory tricks is to add a beautiful stone brooch or even a cluster of them to a basic black dress, T-shirt, sweater, or coat. The visual luxury this adds makes a ten-dollar item look like a two-hundred-dollar item in seconds flat. But jewelry not only adds a layer of luxury, it also adds a layer of femininity and certainty to your ensemble.

Strong, eye-catching pieces that aren't fussy make the best fashion statements. Avoid small necklaces with a hundred little components, a brooch that is so small it's lost on a lapel, earrings that wouldn't be missed if you took them off, or anything that is not adding a layer of stylish confidence. Simple, bold accessories give your style backbone and are perceived as more sophisticated and expensive.

Think about your jewelry statements the way you would a diamond ring. Would you rather have one fabulous large stone that reflects the light perfectly and looks elegant or two dozen tiny diamond chips all pressed together to sort of look like a large diamond? For example, the effortless look of large hoop earrings appears far more sophisticated than over-the-top, door-knocker-style earrings that are so

TIPS

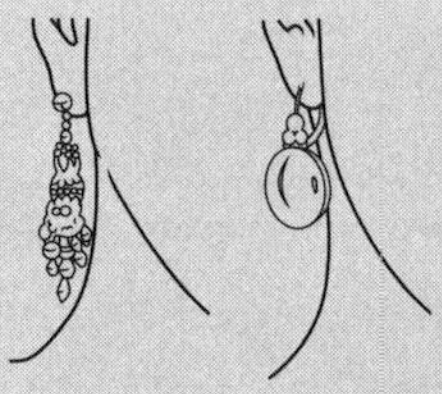

MEDIUM-SIZED DANGLE earrings that are slightly triangular slim your neck, make your jaw look more defined, and make your neck look longer.

detailed they look cheap. When in doubt, opt for jewelry that is simple and larger than you would naturally choose.

Bargain jewelry can be found everywhere—in department stores, thrift stores, yard sales, and flea markets, on eBay, and even at the 7-Eleven. Some of my best accessory buys were found while on vacation in other countries. If your eyes are open to the opportunities, you will find them. Be adventurous, be bold, and get ready for all the compliments.

FAN–BELT

Big-buckled, tied, snapped, at-the-waist, low-slung, through the loops, or on top of it all—your middle is where it's at. The power of the waist is one of our most influential tools, as explained in Chapter 1, and showcasing your hourglass is another of the five key elements of looking great every day.

Now, before you sigh at the thought of highlighting a possibly poochy middle, know that fuller figures can pull off beautiful belts by wearing them on top of a blouse or shirt and under a jacket.

Remember from Chapter 3, this look works because the jacket stunts the visual span of the belt, so you see only the

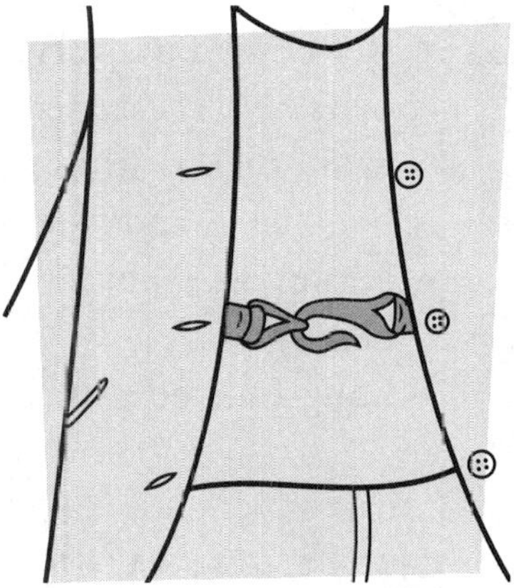

center portion. This bisects the tummy and offers definition at the waist. More slimming than you thought, huh? This is a great option for fuller figures and offers another visual layer of style. So if your tummy is the problem, a strategically placed belt under a blazer will slim that pooch and help create the illusion of a great hourglass.

BEFORE SPORTING your new belt, make sure the "girls" are high enough to showcase your waist! Belts require high boobies.

Buckle Up

Wearing either wide or thin belts over tops, cardigan sweaters, blazers, jackets, and even coats at the tiniest part of your waist is a modern, feminine expression. Again, it is all about creating shape through the waist. Remember these tips when considering strapping one on:

- Choose colorful, rich-looking, expressive belts that have personality, and avoid belts that look too plain and masculine.
- If the shirt requires tucking in, add a belt that makes a statement and fits the size of the belt loops of the pants.

- If you tend to carry your weight in your upper body, belts help create shape and balance the lower body, but avoid tucking things in. Keep tops hemmed to your hip bone area, and wear belts that hit at your natural waist.
- Petites and short-waisted ladies should choose thinner belts.
- Long-waisted gals should sport thicker belts.

FIFTEEN WAYS TO LOVE SCARVES

Adding a scarf to your outfit is a great way to bring several colors together and create fashion flair. I love to take a colorful scarf and use it to coordinate colors and items that I would have never put together otherwise. These little feminine strips of fabric allow you to optimize your wardrobe on a whole new level. Additionally, they pull focus to your beautiful face and look very chic!

You can find bargain scarves everywhere—discount stores, consignment shops, thrift stores, and ethnic enclaves—and you probably have a dozen or more that you have collected over the years and never wear. Why not wear them? Is it because you don't know how? Well, it is time to take them out of the drawer and hang them in your closet so that they are visible—you'll be much more apt to wear them. Now, I'm going to show you fifteen fabulous ways to love scarves:

1. Head scarf: This is very chic with jeans, tank tops, and sandals on the weekend. Simply capture your hair with a

wide scarf, and tie it by one ear. Or take a large square scarf, fold it once to create a triangle, apply the flat side to your forehead, and tie the triangle end down with the two side pieces.

2. Cowl neck: This style looks great and feminizes crewneck tops. Simply take a square scarf, make a triangle, keep the tip of the triangle in your chest, and wrap the ends around and knot in the front. Fold the tip of the triangle under, and fluff. You can also let the ends hang untied for a more voluminous look.

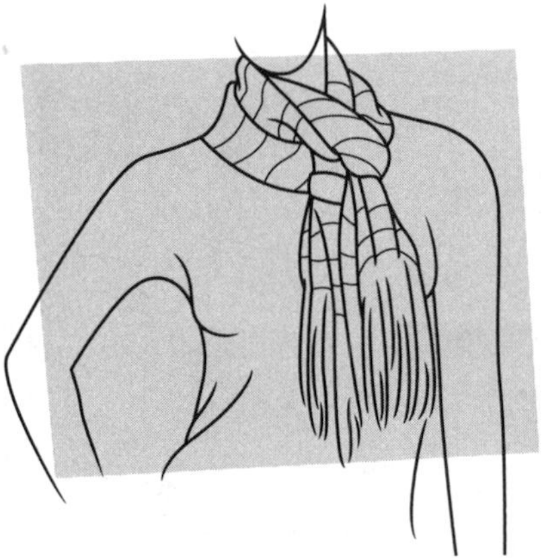

3. Loop: This is a quick and easy way to wear long silk and winter scarves. Put the ends together, making a loop, wrap around your neck, and slip the ends through the loop. Very chi-chi European!

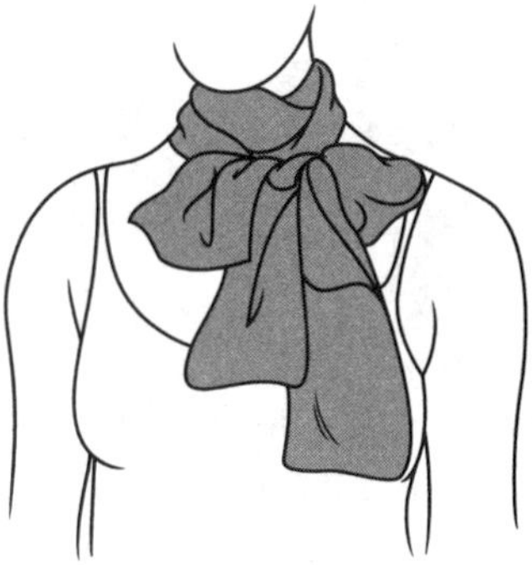

4. Bow: This style adds an elegant touch to basic blouses and tops. Take a long scarf, make a bow, and fluff. Love it!

5. Headband: A beautiful style for the summer, this adds a layer of sophistication and keeps your hair off your face. Take a large scarf, and fold it to about an inch wide. Create a tight headband around your head, and tie underneath or at one ear. Open the ends for a more sophisticated look.

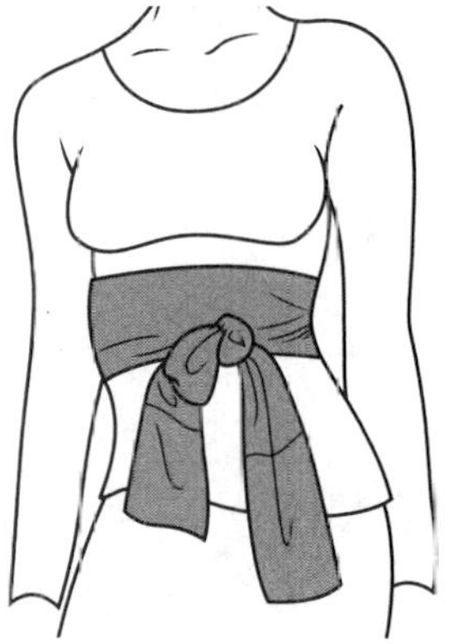

6. Obi: Scarves in heavier silk look beautiful when worn over simple shirts and tied in an obi style. Start with the center of the scarf in the front, wrap around your back, and tie in a square knot on the side. This also looks great with high-waisted pencil skirts and tucked blouses.

7. Wrap: A pashmina-type wrap is a must for every wardrobe. These wraps are perfect for special occasions and offer a feminine layer with sundresses on cool summer nights.

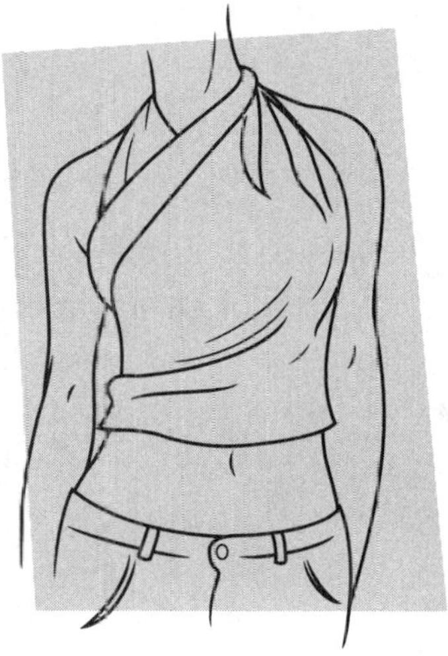

8. Halter: Large square scarves make beautiful halter tops for Caribbean holidays or elegant pool parties. Fold into a triangle, and start with the point at your back. Bring the ends under your arms, wrap across your chest, and tie behind your neck.

9. Belt: Long scarves make unique belts that add a layer of style and texture to basic pieces.

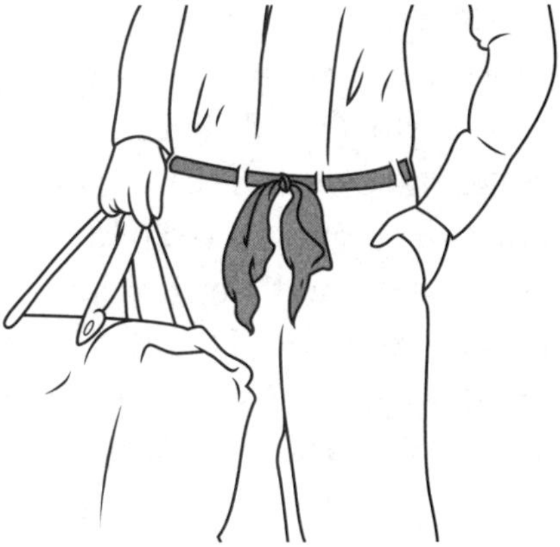

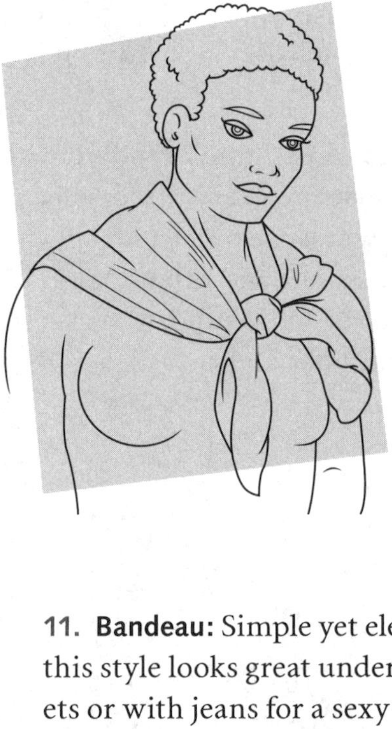

10. Neckerchief: This style is great for ladies with narrow shoulders. It adds lightweight texture, pattern, and layers, offering visual balance. Secure with a simple square knot.

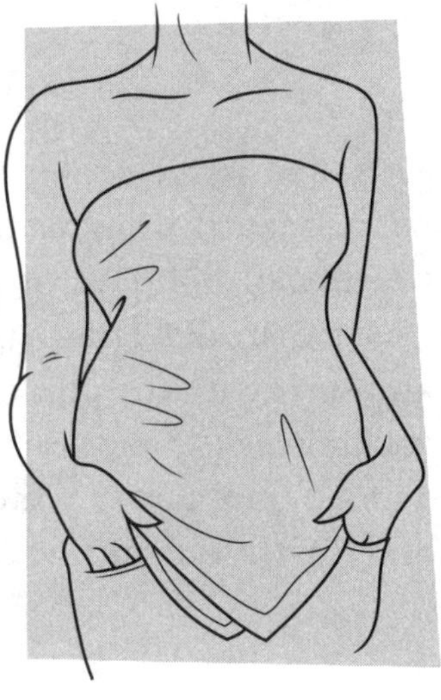

11. Bandeau: Simple yet elegant, this style looks great under jackets or with jeans for a sexy night out. Fold a square scarf into a triangle, place the point at your waist, and tie in the back.

12. Skinny wrap: A long, skinny scarf wrapped once around the neck elongates the body, making you look taller and slimmer.

13. Untied: An elegant square scarf loosely folded and tied takes the place of a blouse and creates an effortless, polished look.

14. Man's tie: As a feminine twist on a masculine knot, I like to wear the scarf close to the skin and not on top of a blouse. Tie as you would a man's slipknot tie.

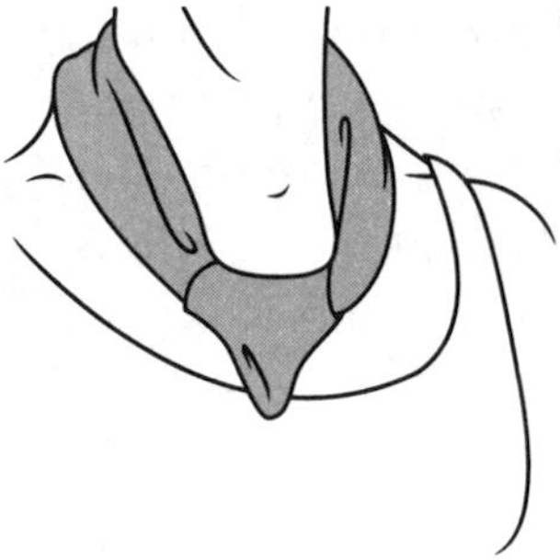

15. Triangle knot: Small bandana-size scarves create interesting necklaces when you fold them tight, make a pretty knot in the front, and then tie them around your neck.

Bonus: Add an elegant scarf to a straw hat for sophisticated Hamptons glamour!

HOT FRAMES FOR YOUR PEEPERS

The coolest accessories on earth are eyeglasses. They are immediate visual indicators of your personality. I mean, glasses are one of the first things that you see when you look at someone, and cool glasses speak volumes during that first impression. I just love glasses, and the selections have never been more hip and affordable.

I recommend you find the pair of eyeglasses that makes you feel super cool and a little edgy when you wear them. Then you will relish having them on. Avoid the mousy basic pair of glasses that say nothing about you and "match everything"; instead, try something new. A strong, angular pair of glasses commands more respect and frames your eyes in a way that adds a visual layer of confidence and authority. Bolder frames are actually known to drive the fellas wild. It's that whole sexy-secretary thing, and who doesn't wanna play that with the right fella?

My favorite bargain tip for finding unusual and unique glasses that speak volumes about your style is to look for antique frames at flea markets and antique malls. Older frames were made of much better materials, and the retro styles were so cool. Quite often, you can find great-looking antique frames for under twenty bucks, and then you take them to your local one-hour eyeglass store for an eye exam and lenses. I speak from experience that this little bargain trick can save you hundreds on the cost of *unique* frames, and everyone will think you are so fashion forward!

Here are some basic rules to consider when selecting those spectacular spectacles:

- Larger faces need larger frames; small faces take smaller ones.
- Dark frames make the face look smaller.
- Light-colored frames emphasize the face as it is.
- Thinner, more delicate frames flatter a small face.
- Big, bold frames are best for larger women.
- Tops of frames should hit around the brow area.

The shape of the frames or unframed lenses should be chosen to correspond to the shape of your face. Oval faces hit the genetic jackpot when it comes to frame options, because everything looks good on an oval mug if no individual features need special consideration. But here are some guidelines:

- Round faces look best with straight, squared-off frames, because they give the face more interesting planes and angles.
- Square faces with a sharp jaw and angular lines are softened by round lenses.
- Heart-shaped faces look best with darker frames that fit close to the head. This will balance a narrow jaw.
- A long face looks best with large frames with strong horizontal lines. They will help the face appear shorter.

When you are shopping for frames, take someone with you, and have him or her use a digital camera to take your picture in the array of frames you're considering. The perspective of looking at your image in the camera's display window really helps you narrow down the frames that best suit your face, and you can easily scroll through the shots to save what you like and delete what you don't like.

Remember that the rules of face shape and frame size apply to sunglasses as well, but there is much more wiggle room when considering a ten-dollar pair of sunglasses versus a hundred-dollar pair of prescription glasses. Sunglasses are a different type of style statement, and they require that more of your eye is covered for protection.

Sunglasses are an individual expression, and most of them look great on most women. The one thing I will warn you against is choosing frames that are too slim, wrap around the face, and look psychedelic or buglike. These glasses tend to take on a costume feel and rarely look chic. Avoid the Devo shades, and opt for something Jackie O would wear, for a classic, fail-proof look.

UNDERWHELM VERSUS OVERKILL

One of the many things I've learned while working in women's closets all across the country is that women love accessories, but they either don't know how to accessorize or are scared to try. Accessorizing is an art form. Learning to scatter your style statements in a strong, feminine way without overdoing it takes a little practice. Quite often, women either under- or overaccessorize, never finding the right balance. This is the very reason I created monthly Cents of Style Accessory Suites (thrifty-chic accessories all bundled together for an immediate style boost—go to centsofstyle .com and check them out).

In the world of graphic arts and interior decorating, you learn the power of color placement and the skill of directing the eye. In the art of accessorizing, you want to employ very similar strategies without causing visual clutter or vacancy. You want to accessorize in such a way that your eye naturally moves from style point to style point. For example, when someone greets you, ideally you want the visual flow to coast from your eyeglasses to a necklace to a belt, and then to handbag and shoes. Or have the eye travel from great earrings to a shoulder bag, a bundle of bracelets on one arm, one playful cocktail ring on the opposite hand, and down to super-cute shoes.

What you want to avoid is strong earrings with oversized glasses, a necklace, bracelets, watch, rings, oversized belt, handbag, and colorful shoes. We all *know* this look and a woman who wears it, Madame D'Bo Coup Accessory. We have someone in our life like this, or we have come across a lady like this, and she quite often frightens us into underaccessorizing or, worse, making wimpy accessory choices. She jingle jangles when she walks, and she comes off as a little flaky and undecided. It seems like she can't edit her style hardware, so she just wears it all at one time.

Christina Aguilera and her "Dirrty"/"Lady Marmalade" phase circa 2000 is a perfect example of a Madame D'Bo Coup Accessory—yikes! No one wants to look like a jacked-up gypsy; it just kind of happens, so the skill of accessory editing is a crucial one.

When accessorizing, remember that two strong statements are plenty, whether they be a scarf and earrings, a bold printed top and layered bangles, a gathering of brooches and earrings, and so on. Never wear bold earrings, necklace, and bracelets, scarf, belt, etc.; pick one or two, and go with it. Accessorize with small, understated earrings and chunkier/layered necklaces, or with larger earrings, no necklace, and bold bracelets. If you have a fabulous wide belt, skip the necklace, and just wear more-noticeable earrings.

Striking the right balance comes with understanding what you want to draw attention to. There are times when

Tips

TRY LAYERING your necklaces of varying lengths, weights, and textures for an unexpected look that puts a new twist on your old stuff!

an outfit is all about a kickin' pair of shoes, and when that's the case, bracelets and belts make the perfect complementary accessories because they guide the eye down to your tootsies. Scarves and earrings are a great combination for those wanting to detract from tummies and tushies. The pattern of a scarf and movement of earrings keep the focus on the upper body and eyes, while the lower body becomes less significant.

Once you have chosen your strong accessory statements, you don't have to ignore or not wear other accessories that you would naturally wear, such as a watch or handbag. You just choose more coordinating, quieter pieces that seemed

Uh, Don't Do That

JUST LIKE genie pants and jelly shoes, it is time to retire the scrunchie. Great modern ponytails are easy to create with just a fabric-covered elastic. The key is to have height at the crown and keep the ponytail at about ear level. Set the scrunchies free . . . let them run free!

more subtle and don't fight for style attention. Remember, two strong statements, and the rest should complement and not detract!

MAKE A STATEMENT

Your accessories tell the world who you are. Think about it. When you see a pristine lady with hair pulled back and sharp, simple clothes, carrying a structured handbag and wearing a strand of pearls, delicate diamond stud earrings, and basic pumps, you know who she is. When you gaze with a smile at the lady in the grocery store who is sporting a food-color-dyed macaroni necklace, running shoes, and a floppy purse big enough to hold a medicine cabinet and a half dozen juice boxes, you know who she is. When the smell of patchouli oil hits you, and you turn to see a wise and beautiful earth mother with a crystal prominently displayed around her neck, a feather delicately dangling from one tiny braid in her hair, and a macramé handbag draped across her body and resting on one hip, you know who she is, too. The accessories we wear simply reflect our spirit and our priorities.

So think about these things when you are getting dressed, shopping, and making choices about your image. Have fun adding flair to your wardrobe, and enjoy hunting and gathering the accessories that let you shine. They certainly don't have to be expensive, but you owe it to yourself to make them fabulous.

Special-Occasion Dressing on a Budget

10

Dressing for a special occasion can be stressful and can even take away from the fun of the occasion itself. We've all been there: we want to go to an event but suffer agony over not having the right thing to wear. (Eeek!) Whether you're on your way to a wedding, a night out after work, a prom, or a weekend getaway, this chapter will make sure you look great for your big event without spending big money. And once you have your wardrobe workforce in place, the stomach-churning unease of not having something to wear will never plague you again.

FINDING *THE* PERFECT PENNY-PINCHING DRESS

Nothing really says special occasion better than a dress, so when events arise, most of us want a new one. But finding *the* perfect dress for a special occasion can be tough when a strong Cents of Style is required.

Like it or not, you need to prepare to try on a gazillion different styles and colors. Employ your Cents of Style shopping strategies, but veer into regular-price territory until you find a style you like. Even if you think you are going to hate it, just try it. What doesn't look good on the hanger can sometimes look beautiful once your body fills it out. This is a great exercise in perspective.

You shouldn't buy anything until you have firmly determined what looks best on you. Special-occasion dresses simply fit differently, and the fabrics and details create different effects, so trial and error in this arena is crucial. Often the style or color that you would have never picked looks the most dynamic. Once you have an idea of the style and color that look best, then focus on getting that combination at a price you can afford.

When you know the type of dress that rocks your world, a great place to purchase your special-occasion dress is over the Internet. Ordering dresses online allows you to easily comparison shop for the best buys and will often allow you to order the dress and color you like, which might not be available in your local store.

When searching, check out sites that offer bridesmaid dresses as well as prom dresses. You may find that the same exact dress will be cheaper when it's listed as a bridesmaid dress as opposed to a prom dress or special-occasion dress. Be sure to err on the larger side. It is much easier to have a dress taken in than to have it let out, and special-occasion dresses are notoriously cut sparingly.

How about some inventive vintage? Depending on the event, perhaps a prom or social reception, thrift stores, resale boutiques, and secondhand stores like the Salvation Army are great places to find slightly used dresses with lots of potential. And don't forget grandparents, parents, and various aunts and cousins. Everyone I know has a gown or two in the back of her closet, vintage or not, so it doesn't hurt to inquire. Ask relatives for a tour of their closet, and keep an eye out for vintage clothing and accessories; also be sure to check out their jewelry boxes while you are visiting. Your grandmother or great-aunt may have a pair of earrings or a cocktail ring that would look amazing with your dress. Not to mention, you'll have something unique.

Fit

Dresses can be a tough fit. When you think about it, a dress has to incorporate the fit elements of two garments in one. The top and the skirt need to fit properly, and the proportions need to work for your figure. The measurements from your shoulder to your waist, from your waist to your knee, plus your bust and hip measurements, all have to work with the dress, or you get an ill-fitted sack that doesn't serve your gorgeous shape.

To be honest, this fit issue is exactly why many dresses end up on the sale rack first in discount stores and in consignment shops all over the country. We often can't put our finger on what we don't like about a dress—it just doesn't fit right—so it doesn't get purchased, or it gets purchased and then used only once or twice. For this reason, dresses offer the biggest bargain opportunities, because you now know how to take a bargain garment and turn it into a stylish stunner for you and your shape. It's all about the tailoring.

In Chapter 6, I laid out how tailoring makes a cheapy look like a cherry, and all of those principles go doubly for special-occasion dresses. When shopping for a dress, of course go to the sale rack first, but again, once you know the styles and colors that look best on you, zero in on the price. A dress of any kind will almost always need tailoring for a great fit, so if you approach your shopping with this understanding, you can take advantage of the best bargains.

Discount stores and consignment shops offer a harvest of dress options. Most people try on a dress and expect everything to fit perfectly, and if it doesn't, they put it back. Well, the bad news for them is the good news for you, because you know better. You are much better off buying a fifty-dollar special-occasion dress and investing thirty dollars in alterations than buying an eighty-dollar dress and having it not fit well. That altered fifty-dollar bargain will look like ten times the price when it fits your body properly, so shop with this understanding. The perfect penny-pinching dress will be found on the sale rack but created at the tailor's shop.

Here are a few general fit tips that can help narrow your search when looking for that perfect dress:

- **Curvy figures** often look best in dresses that accentuate the positives. Try on halter-top styles and corseted styles, as these will naturally offer more shape and/or structure. Consider an A-line skirt that skims the hips and highlights a smaller waist. You don't want to select anything too clingy or glittery, as these can be less forgiving. You want something in a heavier fabric that drapes and doesn't hug the body.

- **Petite figures** can look stunning in shorter tea-length styles, which can help make you appear taller. Ruched bodices are also great for creating more volume up top, and detailed bodices work to pull the focus up, creating the illusion of height.

- **Taller, thin figures** look beautiful in sheath, bias-cut dresses that emphasize the curves while still looking graceful and not hoochie.

Always the Bridesmaid

"Oh, I chose this dress because I thought you could wear it again!" How many times have we heard that one? Yes, you are right; I am dying to wear a peach taffeta gown with a butt bow to my next cocktail party. Thank you for being so considerate.

Truth is, most bridesmaid dresses can be retooled—re-created, if you will—to become a functioning part of your wardrobe. In fact, these garments represent your wardrobe capital, so you owe it to yourself as a thrifty diva to think about how you can get your money's worth out of these often hideous fashionable acts of love and support.

The first step in re-creating a bridesmaid dress is to simplify it as much as you can. Remove all of the froufrou bells, bows, and adornment. Think about how the dress can be stripped so that it can function as an anchor piece, a classically cut garment with little adornment in a fabric you can wear all year long (see Chapter 6). If the structure of the dress offers a flattering shape, you can easily cut it off to the knee, remove dating details, and make it more functional by adding your own accessories as the occasion dictates.

If the top or the skirt of the dress is especially atrocious, consider cutting off the yucky part and creating a usable separate. This trick also works when you outgrow one part of the dress or the other. If the top of the dress offers elegant details but the skirt is pulling across the seat, cut it off, and wear the top with a new skirt or great trousers. If you have enough fabric, use the skirt to create a matching wrap, sash, or headband. If the top is hopeless but the skirt offers sophisticated potential, keep the skirt, and re-create a feminine anchor piece.

Another relatively easy optimizer is to try to dye the dress black. Depending on the fabric and design of the dress, a three-dollar box of Rit dye may just salvage that two-hundred-dollar maroon monstrosity after all. Matte fabrics with little or no shine work best for this re-creation trick.

The point is to think about the workable elements of the dress. You probably spent a lot on the darn thing, and more than likely, there is a way to utilize the basic elements. A great knee-length dress, skirt, or fancy top will always bolster your wardrobe and see you ready for the next special occasion. So don't bury these dresses in the back of your closet; honor your wardrobe capital. With just a little effort, a Donate can become a useful Re-Create.

DAY TO EVENING LIKE A SHOPPER HERO

Is it even possible to think about adding one more time commitment to your day? If you knew you could look totally fabu at that social function scheduled for Tuesday at 6:00 P.M., would you go? Well, it's absolutely possible. Now that you have your wardrobe workforce and know that tops and accessories are going to set the mood of an outfit, a daytime data-entry dame can become a dramatic dining diva as quickly as Clark Kent becomes Superman in a phone booth.

Let's talk about what elements and details make for special-occasion dressing. First, as a general rule, the more removed your heels are from the floor, generally the more special the occasion, so a feminine pair of high heels is a must. Second, evening events call for a little sparkle, so whether it is in a wrap, a sequined top, rhinestone earrings, or a metallic evening bag, you want to incorporate a little bling. Femininity is essential, and a little drama is what makes the whole thing fun.

But another key ingredient in making your evening look work and seem less officy is the fabric of your anchor pieces. Evening pieces have more flow and seem more slinky and sleek. Wool is not an evening fabric, and thicker fabrics in general aren't. So when you're considering these elements—heels, sparkle, femininity, flow, and drama—here is how you can easily pull off this transition.

When deciding what to wear for your day at work, think about a sexy dress that has movement and is cut to the knee; wear it under a structured jacket. Add a brooch to the jacket and a thin pashmina (wrap-type) scarf for more décolleté coverage. Wear the scarf loop style as illustrated in Chapter 9. In your work tote, carry a strappy pair of heels and an

REMEMBER, HOSIERY is no longer a necessity for special occasions, especially when you're sporting beautiful strappy sandals. If hosiery is a requirement at the office, free yourself from the nylon bondage before you slide into your party slippers.

evening bag filled with chandelier earrings, a cocktail ring, a pretty bracelet, and bobby pins.

Come 5:01 P.M., take off that jacket, add the brooch to the side of a tousled updo, exchange your day jewelry for the special stuff stashed in your evening bag, and add strappy heels to bare legs and a cute pedicure. If needed, use the pashmina as a wrap.

When transitioning a pantsuit from day to night, choose a black suit with modern-fitting pants—nothing tapered and preferably something extra long, so you can just peep your hot strappy-clad toes out from the hemline. Again, a medium-weight fabric, something that can be worn all year long, will serve you best for this transition.

If you choose a dark suit with a tailored, well-fitted jacket—something simple without casual details like top stitching, excessive buttons, booby pockets, etc.—you can easily pull this off as an evening tuxedo look when it's paired with the right top. I would recommend you pack your work tote with a sequined or silky camisole, a cluster of rhinestone brooches (a least three that coordinate with each other to create a strong visual statement) or a beautiful silk flower pin, a few strands of long pearls, strappy high-heeled sandals, and a metallic evening bag.

When the work whistle blows, replace your demure work top with the sexy, slinky cami, and add either brooches or the flower pin to your lapel. The long, layered pearls will offer a chic touch, adding movement and elegance to your work suit, and the combination of pins and pearls sell the look as a Chanel runway stunner.

Keep the earrings tiny, as you will be sporting enough visual detail on your lapel. You can add one elegant cocktail ring if you would like, but the flower pin or brooch cluster will probably be enough bling. Your evening bag and strappy sandals will further feminize this sexy tuxedo look as effortless and glamorous. Voilà!

EVENING MAKEUP can easily be achieved with a little more intensity. Add an extra layer of mascara and a touch more eyeliner, and deepen the accent colors of your eye shadow. If time doesn't allow, the quickest way to add immediate drama to your evening face is to apply a coat of red lipstick. Nothing says glamour like a crimson pucker.

One more great way to pull off the day to night glamourama transition is with a classic crisp white shirt. Sharon Stone at the Oscars in the late nineties and Drew Barrymore at numerous Hollywood premieres have showcased how a beautiful crisp white blouse can look timelessly elegant and downright *hot*! The key to this rich look is to take the basic white cotton blouse and make it sexy. Again, you need a slinky feminine anchor piece, be it wide-leg trousers with movement, a pencil skirt that hugs your frame, or a full skirt that creates a perfect hourglass; you have to feel sexy in what you are pairing with your basic white blouse to pull off this evening-chic look.

However you wear your crisp, perfectly fitted white blouse to work, when party time arrives, you want to unbutton the blouse as low as possible and reveal a lace cami or the hint of a fashionable bra. Now, before you gasp:

the peekaboo of a deliberately coordinating bra is both sexy and appropriate. It is no more risqué than a strapless dress, so rehinge your jaw.

I actually like to unbutton the blouse completely, flip up the collar and wrap-tuck the shirt tails into my bottoms for a body-conscious effect that creates a beautiful new elongating neckline.

The accessories take center stage here again, as a bright-colored wide belt, layered beads or pearls that fall inside the collar, and an effortless updo with stud earrings make you the belle of the after-work ball. For an extra punch, coordinate sexy colored pumps or high-heeled sandals and an evening bag with the color of your wide belt.

With a well-fitted wardrobe workforce and a collection of fabulous accessories, you never have to say no to a party. Besides, a Wednesday-night bash makes the week seem shorter!

APPROPRIATE OR HOOEY?

The thought that you can't wear pants, boots, and patterned prints to a special occasion is just plain hooey! Pants can be a very elegant option when you employ all the fit and fabric principles. For that matter, elegant palazzo pants (pants with a super-wide leg) are a statuesque option that creates beautiful flow and movement.

When choosing palazzo pants for a special occasion, it is imperative that you get the right length and fit through the thigh. The pant legs should barely graze the floor when you walk, and nothing should cling at the thigh, to truly capture the richness of this look. Because of the extreme anchoring volume of palazzo pants, you want to keep your tops simple and somewhat body-conscious for proportion and balance.

For years, boots were considered too casual to wear to a special event or cocktail reception, but that rule has been squashed as well. Additionally, boots are not just for fall or winter events; they can be worn well into spring, depending on the climate where you live. Sleek pointed-toe, stiletto-heel, or kitten-heel knee boots can be a very dressed-up option when paired with matching opaque tights. I have even added a brooch to chic suede boots for a touch of ritzy bling.

The look of opaque tights and elegant boots gives you the fashion license to wear hemlines just a little bit shorter, because you are more covered up. So a simple brightly colored silk mini sheath dress found on the sale rack for under thirty bucks can be brought into sophisticated balance with dark opaque tights, elegant knee boots, a long dropped rhinestone pendant necklace, complementing evening bag, and sleek hair.

In the same way you tamed a brightly colored dress with dark, elegant boots, you can temper luxurious prints, making them perfect for a special occasion. A beautiful patterned print dress or top should be offset by basic accessories and understated pieces so that the print is not visually fighting for attention, becoming the wow factor of your special-occasion ensemble.

If you find a beautiful scarf print dress at a thrift store, don't try to match your accessories to one of the colors in the dress; match them to the background color, for a richer look when attending a special occasion. Use your accessories to push attention to the print and not away from it, and you will be big-night ready.

And speaking of accessories, as always, your accessories will set the mood and tone of your special-occasion ensemble. But bad accessorizing can also make you look like a reject from a cheesy casino show! Give your gorgeous dress or ensemble a good long gander, and think about what additional sparkle will pull it all together without seeming overdone.

Keep in mind, as explained in Chapter 9, that more than two strong accessory statements will send you on your way to tacky town. You never want to wear a bold necklace, bold earrings, and a bold bracelet and carry a heavily detailed handbag. You need to scatter your accessory statements. Think about this:

- If your outfit has a lot of detail like beading, sequins, appliqués, or rhinestones on the bodice, avoid a necklace that would detract from that detail. Choose stronger dangle earrings and a bracelet instead.

- If your outfit has a simple top with detail on the skirt, choose a beautiful necklace and smaller, not so matchy-matchy earrings. A bold necklace with bold earrings is always overkill.

- If your outfit is more basic, punch it up with a dazzling handbag and chandelier earrings. Or choose a bold necklace and stunning bracelet. Once you have chosen your two key accessories, your other choices should be minimal and support the look and tone of your featured pieces.
- If your outfit has lots of razzle-dazzle, keep the accessories simple and free of excessive detail. Let your ensemble stand alone!

SPECIAL OCCASIONS call for attention to detail. Nails, hair, makeup, and accessories all work to create a special look that reflects the importance of an event. If you have chosen beautiful open-toed sandals, make sure your toenails are polished and your heels are not cracked. Even if you don't have time for an official pedicure, slap some color on your toes, and moisturize your feet so that they look subtle. Crusty feet and chipped polish can ruin an otherwise flawless look, so don't step out without checking your steppers.

SEXY VERSUS INAPPROPRIATE

Now here comes a subject I have been dying to write about, because it seems like we have all lost our ever-lovin' minds when it comes to putting ourselves on parade. With celebs flashing their hoo-has, half-draped boobies flaunted like winning cakes at a bakeoff, and tattooed coin slots peeking out of bent-over britches, one has got to ask, "What qualifies as inappropriate anymore?"

There is a general rule of thumb when considering something sexy: it is best to pick one area of allure and feature that. Too much skin is not a good thing, even when considering evening events. But before I go further, let me be clear: I want you to dress sexily and feel sexy. When you feel sexy, you naturally radiate a confidence that is very powerful. But sexy really starts in your head, not on your body.

When dressing sexily for any occasion, remember the female form itself is sexy. It is the most provocative shape there is. Showcasing your curves with fabric that drapes your body can be much more captivating than overexposing yourself. Work your curves instead.

Remember that incredible navy-blue gown Hilary Swank wore to the Oscars in 2005? She was covered up to her neck with just the perfect skin of her back exposed, but the draping on her beautiful form was breathtaking. She made a choice to reveal one part of her and make a demure yet alluring fashion statement that was very sexy. Charlize Theron is also a master of this captivating trick. Whenever you see her in a minidress, it is topped with a turtleneck and long sleeves, visually pushing the focus to her beautiful legs and creating a sexy statement that is appropriate and not over the top.

That is the key: If you are going to wear the miniskirt, you can't opt for the strapless top. If you are working the cleavage, cover your gams to the knee. A message of subtlety will always be perceived as a powerful fashion expression of self-confidence and not attention-getting desperation. (Take note, Ms. Spears!)

So find your sexy balance. Pick a part you like—your best asset, if you will—and work that with ladylike flair. Anything else teeters on inappropriate and will look cheap. This balance will visually elevate your outfit, no matter how much you paid for it, and give it a much more sophisticated, richer appeal.

PACKING FOR A THREE-DAY GETAWAY

I didn't want to finish the book without addressing a question I get hundreds of e-mails about: packing. Efficient and fashionable packing for travel is an art, and as you build your wardrobe and follow all of my Cents of Style tips, you will start to develop an eye for how to put things together and make your wardrobe workforce multitask for you on the road. But I thought I would offer a little guidance to jump-start the development of your packing talents. I want to give you an example of how an effective wardrobe of anchor pieces, tops, and accessories can easily be pulled together for style-filled travel that is hassle free.

Anytime is the perfect time to sneak off for a quick three-day getaway in the sun or on the winter slopes, and packing light is essential to the fun and spontaneity of it all! Packing your bag is just like building your wardrobe; you want to start with your wardrobe workforce and then choose tops and accessories that allow you to do double or triple duty with those key pieces. Here are some easy tips to keep you contained to one bag, looking fabulous and ready for anything.

Fun in the Sun

- Choose a color story (such as white/khaki, black/red, turquoise/brown, gray/yellow) for all of your garments, so everything will coordinate and you can pack fewer shoes and accessories.

- Fabrics should be wash-and-wear, wrinkle-free options that can be hand washed with a little baby shampoo if need be.

- Every garment packed should serve a dual purpose or be able to be dressed up and dressed down. For example, a flirty skirt should function as a casual skirt with a tank and flip-flops for souvenir shopping and as a dressier dinner option with heels and a sexy top. A colorful wrap should serve as a sarong for your bathing suit at the beach, a night-time wrap for sun-kissed shoulders, and a blankie on the plane. Bermuda shorts should be worn with walking shoes and tanks for sightseeing, then later with strappy heels and a flirty top for a night out.

- Allow yourself three pairs of shoes max. You should travel in a modern feminine walking shoe; pack a strappy heel for night and a sophisticated (nonrubber) flip-flop for relaxing daytime activities.

- Pack hair accessories such as a modern headband and/or scarf to maintain an easy, stylish look that will limit primp time and optimize playtime!

- Choose a refined tankini swimsuit, so you can wear the top with coordinating cropped pants or skirt.

- Choose strategic accessories that will dictate the mood of your outfit.

So, in a thrifty-chic carry-on, you should pack these items:

- Skirt
- Bermuda shorts
- One colorful tank top
- One flow-y, sexy top
- Tankini bathing suit
- Crushable sun hat
- Scarf or headband
- Sophisticated flip-flops
- Strappy heels
- Sparkly chandelier earrings
- Small clutch evening bag
- A thin nighty
- Undies
- Zip-out travel bag for beach, shopping, and souvenirs

You should travel in these items:

- Cropped pants
- Tank top
- Lightweight hoodie
- Modern feminine walking shoe
- Colorful wrap (worn as a scarf and to be used as a blankie when needed)
- Statement watch
- Hoop earrings
- Sunglasses
- A great coordinating tote bag

Winter Whoopee!

- A fitted leather jacket is the foundation of your winter getaway wardrobe. A feminine leather jacket is sexy, tough, fashionable, and functional. The key is to choose something that showcases your waist and ends around your hip bone. Your weekend jacket should not look as if it was stripped from a fighter pilot!

- You want to choose a solid-color heavy wrap that looks great atop your jacket. This will add another layer of warmth to your day and night looks as well as serve as a great blankie on the plane.

- Once again, committing to a color story will save you time and space in your carry-on. Winter scarves are a great place to start when choosing a color story, because they are such a fun, cozy accessory that's the perfect fashion topper for all of your weekend looks.

- It is best to choose lightweight layering tops, as opposed to a sack of bulky sweaters. Body-hugging long-sleeved tees with scoop necklines and thin body-loving turtlenecks offer more warmth and femininity when layered than one big sweater. Warmth and comfort never mean you have to sacrifice style and femininity, so choose your pieces wisely.

- Sophisticated jeans play a big part in a wintertime getaway. You want to choose a dark boot-cut jean that can be dressed up with high-heeled boots and tucked into casual boots for the day.

- A button-up cardigan, hoodie, or versatile sweater jacket that zips is essential. These pieces are much better for layering than a pullover sweater and allow for a more figure-flattering ensemble.

- A slinky matte-jersey dress (Ms. Diane von Furstenberg–esque) that falls above the knee is the perfect choice for a wrinkle-free evening out when added to opaque tights, sexy knee-high boots, and long, layered necklaces. The shorter length then makes the dress a fun, fashionable statement when worn over a paper-thin turtleneck with heavy leggings and your casual boots for day.

- Take two pairs of knee-high boots—one flat, casual pair to be worn during the day and one sexy pair for hot nights out.

- Don't forget the lace! A lace cami with warm leggings gives you something nice and cozy to sleep in and allows you to add a lacy peekaboo layer to your day and night looks. For example, a great nighttime look would be your dark boot-cut jeans, high-heeled boots, lace cami, layered necklaces, fitted leather jacket, warm wrap, and modern clutch.

- Choose a great beret or cute knit hat to add a layer of style and offer warmth. A cute hat will cut down coif time and make your winter style look effortless.

- Other accessories to round out your looks will include statement earrings; a color-complementing watch; long, layering necklaces for your evening looks; and a larger evening clutch.

So in that fabulous carry-on bag, here's what you should pack:

- A sexy pair of knee-high boots
- A thin body-conscious turtleneck
- A long-sleeved scoopneck tee
- A heavy pair of leggings
- A lace cami
- A short, fun matte-jersey dress
- Opaque tights
- Warm socks
- Undies
- Long necklaces for layering and sparkle at night
- A large clutch handbag
- A zip-out tote for souvenirs and great bargains found while shopping

You should travel in these items:

- Scoopneck long-sleeved tee
- Shapely zip-up sweater or button-up cardigan
- Winter scarf, wrapped flat against the body and tucked into the sweater
- Fitted leather jacket
- Dark, sophisticated jeans
- Casual boots
- Heavy winter wrap
- Chunky colorful watch
- Beret
- Hoop earrings
- Sunglasses
- Great statement tote bag

These travel essentials will have you looking fabulous, not like a typical tourist, and ready for anything over your three-day getaway! And now, the most important tip for any event: *have fun!*

As special occasions and wonderful getaway opportunities arise, there is no need to sweat it. Your fabulous Cents of Style wardrobe filled with amazing anchor pieces, versatile tops, and modern accessories will have you ready for anything and looking incredible every step of the way.

And that is the ultimate goal—to have you armed with the skills, tools, and wardrobe knowledge that put you at ease with the understanding that you can achieve the look you want and enjoy the great style you crave with the budget you have. The unique, confident, stylish woman who lives within us all is ready to be celebrated for her great Cents of Style.

11

It's a Wrap

WELL, NOW YOU have the tools. You know how to shop for great bargains, organize your closet for optimal use, put things together with style and flair, and get yourself in a bra that makes you want to sing to the heavens.

I hope you are energized and excited to take a fresh new look at your old stuff and rethink how you are shopping and dressing. After working with hundreds of women, I'm sure that some readers of this book will be paralyzed with info overload. I get that, so I want to take things down a notch and focus on just changing one thing at a time, so you can make the baby steps that will eventually build to fashionable distinction.

If you tackle just one of these things a day for a couple of weeks, these changes will produce the results that will see you inspired to tackle the bigger challenges. I promise.

JUST CHANGE ONE THING

A personal Cents of Style takes developing style muscles, and all change starts with a first step. You know by now that you don't have to spend a fortune or go crazy shopping for the hottest new ensemble, especially if you have your anchor pieces and wardrobe workforce in order. Staying current and maintaining a pulled-together, modern look can be as easy as just changing one thing. Simply reach for that key item or make one shift that's going to speak volumes.

The fastest and easiest way to add a jolt of fashion electricity to your mundane daily uniform, be it jeans and a tee, gray suits, or scrubs, is with accessories. There is plenty of accessory info in Chapter 9, but I want to offer a few jumping-off places to help get you started on your road to a great Cents of Style.

By adding a vibrant, unexpected accessory, you can quickly and inexpensively transform your look. Consider these simple additions, items you probably have right now, for a major shot of fashion mojo and a great example of how changing just one thing can change everything:

- **Brighten your lipstick!** As you remember, wearing lipstick is one of my five essentials for looking great every day, and brightening your lipstick can inject your whole look with youth. A brighter lipstick brings life to your face and encourages people to listen to what you say as they are attracted to your mouth.

- **Change your bra!** In Chapter 2, I laid out the importance of a great-fitting bra. If there is nothing else you change, let it be your brassiere! This one adjustment can change everything you put on—and even your posture. Don't let tomorrow go by without measuring yourself and making sure you are wearing the right size. A new bra can make you feel like a new woman!

- **Choose a dazzling outer layer.** There is *no* rule that says we have to buy a black or tan coat. I know that we are all concerned with the old rules of "matching," but let's face it, those rules are just that—old. A fabulous coat in a rich color can bring a smile to your face every day and send a message of color courage like nothing else. If it is time for a new coat, consider your favorite color, and go for it. The fortunate part is that the most colorful options usually end up on the sale rack, so you should have no trouble exercising your new thrifty-diva know-how.

- **Forgo the standard black, and opt for colorful shoes.** Shoes can change the look of your outfit immediately, and you would be surprised at how happy a sassy pair of shoes can make you feel. When you are out shopping, push through your ingrained need for another pair of black shoes, and be bold. If you change nothing else but your shoes, you will be high stepping with cute style slippers.

- **Wrap some sunshine around your neck.** We all have scarves, and I have shown you fifteen ways to use them (see Chapter 9), so now take one out of your drawer and wear it! They'll brighten up your whole look. Come on, you can do it!

- **How about a chunky new watch in a fabulous hue?** When you are just starting to build your style muscles and dabble with new and exciting colors, buying a watch in a bright, fun color can be an easy and impactful first step. Every time you look at your watch you are reminded of your color courage, and the compliments will undoubtedly pour in for your spunky new accessory. So hear ye, hear ye! A fabulous yellow watch goes with everything! Now march.

- **Make a statement with a vivid handbag or tote.** A fantastic way to perk up every outfit in your closet and show a little creative flair is by changing your handbag. Basic black is OK but really just that—basic! Why not sport a fabulous red, bright green, or robin's-egg-blue handbag? Everything you wear will look hip and fresh, and you'll feel thrifty chic for updating your entire wardrobe with a single purchase.

- **Add colorful bangle bracelets to a monochromatic look.** A stack of colorful bracelets can offer modern texture and a stylish look to an all-white, an all-black, or a color-blocked outfit. Don't be afraid to mix and match bracelet colors, and remember your Cents of Style Color Formula. When wearing a cool-toned top, choose warm tones for accessories, and vice versa. Bangles are an easy and fashionable way to knock this formula out of the fashion ballpark.

- **Vibrant beads always add retro flavor.** Beads and colorful necklaces are simple, fashionable layering pieces that work to call attention to the good stuff. By adding a strand of beads, you add emphasis to the décolleté and pull attention to your upper body near your face, skin, and eyes. I know you have some beads; why not wear them tomorrow?

- **Strong, dangly statement earrings still convey high style.** Medium-sized to large earrings will always look younger and more fashionable. Smaller, conservative earrings naturally look more mature and generic. As women hit the workforce in the 1970s, they were instructed not to draw attention to themselves with large earrings or accessories. That rule is out of the window, as a strong woman who is sure of her style and power can and should wear whatever she wants. Don't be afraid of a dangle earring, but remember to let that stand alone. No need to add a strong necklace, pin, bangles, and the works. Strong earrings say a lot.

- **Highlight your hourglass with a fabulous belt.** Have you heard enough about how important your waist is? Adding a belt to a basic dress, topping a coat with a wide waist cincher, or giving some rock 'n' roll flair to your jeans with a tough studded belt can all act as a feminine call to the middle. The waist is what makes us girls, so the more we can do to create shape and highlight that curve, the more powerful we look.

- **Replace your pumps with boots.** This one change can make your entire outfit look tougher and more stylish. If you have to wear skirt suits to work every day or if you love dresses but want to give yours an update, opt for a luxurious boot. Boots naturally feel and look young; they also offer a great juxtaposition of masculine roughness with feminine skirts and dresses, creating the stylish intrigue that will set you apart. This one change can change everything.

Remembering to change or add just one thing every day is sure to bear some style fruit. What happens when we take fashion risks is that people notice. More often than not, we are encouraged and receive compliments on our fashion updates, because people are naturally attracted to new and different things. Through that encouragement, we build more confidence and become more courageous.

These small, risky fashion steps are how we slowly become the expressive, modern dressers we want to be. And the really cool thing is that all of these little changes can be found at thrift stores and consignment shops and on sale racks all over town. No huge investment here—just small thrifty-chic purchases that make a large impact. You are sure to be a shopper hero and expressive thrifty diva in no time.

FINAL THOUGHT

I have something for you to think about. Femininity is at the heart of what I teach and the economical fashion philosophy I believe in. Femininity is quite simply the most powerful thing that we "put on" every day, and it doesn't cost a thing.

As I've crisscrossed the country over the past few years, working with incredible women to create powerful, renewed, thrifty-chic images, the one constant that I've discovered is that most of us think we have to sacrifice femininity for comfort, for respect, for corporate success, or for economical dressing. In fact, appearing more masculine, uncared for, and in denial of the essence of who we are is extremely disempowering and more costly on many levels!

Being comfortable should not and doesn't have to equal more-masculine clothes that hide our shape, more-expensive clothes that offer a false status, or generic clothes that don't express who we are. Consider this: the more strength we draw and express from our feminine core through our dress, makeup, and hair, the more impactful we become. Allowing ourselves the time and space for true expression, without fear of judgment, nurtures our creative core, strengthening us as unique women. Using our wardrobe to become more self-aware, confident, connected, and empowered is what having a great Cents of Style is all about.

I've said it a million times, but there is nothing more comfortable than looking great, and celebrating your womanhood through your image is a gift waiting to be opened every day. Economical, creative, powerful, feminine dressing can change your life. It ignites you to achieve more, accomplish more, communicate more, face more, as you have the assurance of fashionable feminine fabulosity! And in giving yourself the gift of looking radiant every day, you give all those around you permission to do the same.

Be happy! Be beautiful! Be thrifty!

Index

About the Author

Andy Paige is the celebrated Beauty and Style Expert on NBC's Emmy-winning daytime reality drama "Starting Over" and a member of the "Glam Squad" on TLC's "Ten Years Younger." With almost two decades' experience in New York and Los Angeles as a professional fit model, makeup artist, celebrity stylist, writer, broadcaster, and baroness of bargains, Andy has done more than a hundred "frugalicious" makeovers on TV.

Andy is the owner of Cents of Style, a solutions-based image business dedicated to helping women look like a million without spending a fortune. Andy does Beauty Boot Camps with private clients and frequently holds Cents of Style workshops throughout the country. She contributes to *Soap Opera Digest*, the *National Enquirer*, *Woman's Day*, *First*, *Roam*, the *New York Sun*, *Cutting Edge*, and InStyle.com. Visit her website at centsofstyle.com.